MAKING THE MOST OF
ANNUALS
IN THE GARDEN

MAKING THE MOST OF
ANNUALS
IN THE GARDEN

A COMPREHENSIVE VISUAL DIRECTORY AND PRACTICAL
ENCYCLOPEDIA OF ANNUAL PLANTS TO SUIT ALL STYLES
AND EVERY KIND OF OUTDOOR SPACE

RICHARD BIRD

southwater

This edition is published by Southwater, an imprint of Anness Publishing Ltd, Hermes House, 88–89 Blackfriars Road, London SE1 8HA; tel. 020 7401 2077; fax 020 7633 9499

www.southwaterbooks.com; www.annesspublishing.com

If you like the images in this book and would like to investigate using them for publishing, promotions or advertising, please visit our website www.practicalpictures.com for more information.

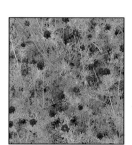

UK agent: The Manning Partnership Ltd; tel. 01225 478444; fax 01225 478440; sales@manning-partnership.co.uk

UK distributor: Grantham Book Services Ltd; tel. 01476 541080; fax 01476 541061; orders@gbs.tbs-ltd.co.uk

North American agent/distributor: National Book Network; tel. 301 459 3366; fax 301 429 5746; www.nbnbooks.com

Australian agent/distributor: Pan Macmillan Australia; tel. 1300 135 113; fax 1300 135 103; customer.service@macmillan.com.au

New Zealand agent/distributor: David Bateman Ltd; tel. (09) 415 7664; fax (09) 415 8892

ETHICAL TRADING POLICY

At Anness Publishing we believe that business should be conducted in an ethical and ecologically sustainable way, with respect for the environment and a proper regard to the replacement of the natural resources we employ.

As a publisher, we use a lot of wood pulp to make high-quality paper for printing, and that wood commonly comes from spruce trees. We are therefore currently growing more than 500,000 trees in two Scottish forest plantations near Aberdeen – Berrymoss (130 hectares/320 acres) and West Touxhill (125 hectares/305 acres). The forests we manage contain twice the number of trees employed each year in paper-making for our books.

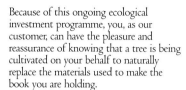

Because of this ongoing ecological investment programme, you, as our customer, can have the pleasure and reassurance of knowing that a tree is being cultivated on your behalf to naturally replace the materials used to make the book you are holding.

Our forestry programme is run in accordance with the UK Woodland Assurance Scheme (UKWAS) and will be certified by the internationally recognized Forest Stewardship Council (FSC). The FSC is a non-government organization dedicated to promoting responsible management of the world's forests. Certification ensures forests are managed in an environmentally sustainable and socially responsible basis. For further information about this scheme, go to www.annesspublishing.com/trees

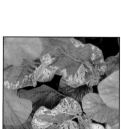

A CIP catalogue record for this book is available from the British Library.

Publisher: Joanna Lorenz
Editorial Director: Helen Sudell
Editor: Rosie Gordon
Designer: Michael Morey
Production Controller: Wendy Lawson

Previously published as part of a larger volume, *Knowing & Growing Annuals & Perennials* and *Annuals* by Richard Bird

10 9 8 7 6 5 4 3 2 1

Contents

INTRODUCTION

In spite of a modern tendency for television personalities to create gardens with few or no plants, there is no doubt in most people's minds that without plants a garden is simply not a garden. There is something about the presence of plants – their colour, shape and fragrance – that lifts the spirits in a very special way. Annuals are extremely popular flowering plants, offering a vast selection of ways to add that vital colour and stimulus to every kind of garden.

Enjoying plants

Plants give pleasure to people in many different ways. The majority of gardeners enjoy filling space with colour, shape and texture as well as planning a garden to make the most of their chosen plants' strong points. There are others for whom it is the plant itself that is of principal interest. They are less interested in how the plant fits into the overall picture of the garden, or indeed how the garden looks as a whole, and are more

Anyone can produce this magnificent array of dahlias, verbenas and salvias. It remains colourful for a long period, from midsummer well into autumn.

absorbed by growing a particular type of plant to absolute perfection. These gardeners may only grow plants in order to show them, or simply because they enjoy the challenge of growing rare and difficult types.

There are others still who garden simply because they enjoy working in the open air and get a real joy from cultivation. For them it is the process as well as the results that matter. The huge variety of annuals and perennials that are available, and the many ways in which they can be grown, can easily cater to all these different approaches.

Starting out

Tackling a large bare patch may seem a rather daunting task to somebody who has not done any gardening before, but it is nothing like as difficult as some experts would have you believe. Gardening is rather like decorating a room: naturally a

certain amount of time and effort is involved, but if you are not satisfied with the result you can always change it. This is particularly true with annual plants as you can start from scratch each year.

Oenothera biennis and *Tanacetum parthenium* produce a fine yellow and white scheme.

This border mixes annuals, hardy perennials and tender perennials treated as annuals.

The sunflower, *Helianthus,* is the most obvious example of an annual that is simple to grow and adds vibrant colour to the garden.

right next year, or even the year after. Having said that, there are, of course, basic sensible and effective practices that have developed over many generations, and these are clearly outlined in this book.

Choosing your plants

Plants form the basis of all good gardens and we have produced a detailed directory which will introduce you to a wide range of the very best annuals.

There are far more annuals available than we could hope to include in this book, but the directory has been specially devised to act as a comprehensive basis. As you develop your garden you will become more interested in certain plants rather than others. You will then be able to create your own database of information from nursery catalogues, magazines, books and the internet. Soon you may even find that you have turned into one of those gardeners for whom studying plants is as fascinating as actually growing them.

Working with colour

Many beginners are worried about combining colours, but the key is simply to go for plants and effects that you like without worrying about what other people do.

Remember that we all have some ability where colour is concerned: we choose what goes with what when we get dressed each day and we choose colours for decorating and furnishing our homes. Planning a garden is really no different. In the same way that there are fashion magazines to help you choose your style, so there is no shortage of different kinds of gardening magazine to browse through for inspiration, and there is nothing more enjoyable than wandering around other people's gardens in search of good ideas.

In the end, no garden's success is thanks to tips or magazines, although these have their place. Gardening is about trial and error.

Learning the ropes

There is also no need to worry about gardening techniques. Most gardening is common sense and if you do make a mistake, just remember that you can always put it

An informal container – featuring annual sweet peas, tender verbenas and perennial violas – demonstrates just how effectively annuals and perennials can be mixed.

What is an Annual?

The definition of an annual is not quite as straightforward as it might seem at first. Fundamentally, annuals are plants that grow and die within one year, but in gardening terms we usually think of them as plants that we use during the course of one year only and then discard, even though they might, in certain conditions, live longer. This means that the definition also encompasses biennial plants as well as a few tender and short-lived perennials.

True annuals

Those plants that grow from seed each year, flower and then die, with only the seeds surviving to the following year, are known as true annuals. Some annuals, such as those used as bedding plants or for containers, such as *Lobelia erinus*, have a very long season and will flower from the beginning of summer right through until the middle or end of autumn. Others, however, such as the amusingly named poached egg plant (*Limnanthes*

Brightly-coloured pelargoniums and mesembryanthemum create a spectacular display when used in this colourful bedding scheme. The scheme is unusual in that it has been created in a rock garden.

douglasii), have a brief but dramatic flowering of perhaps only a couple of weeks or even less. In addition to length of flowering time, there are other many characteristics that help differentiate types of annuals.

Hardy annuals

One of the most useful types of annual, especially for use in mixed plantings, are the hardy annuals. These can be sown directly into the soil or in trays or pots to be planted out in autumn where they will survive the winter unprotected, ready to produce flowers in the late spring or early summer, well before the more tender bedding comes into flower. Forget-me-nots (*Myosotis*) are a good example of this.

Half-hardy annuals

Annuals that are "half-hardy" will not tolerate frost and should be either grown from seed in a greenhouse or conservatory and planted out once the danger of frosts has passed or sown directly into the soil once temperatures are guaranteed to be above freezing. Those sown directly into the soil will flower much later than those that have been raised under glass in the spring and planted out as almost mature plants, and in some cases as fully mature plants in full flower. Anything grown under protection needs to be fully hardened off before it is planted outside. Examples of half-hardy annuals include French marigolds (*Tagetes patula*) and cosmos. Sometimes a distinction is made between half-hardy annuals and tender ones (see below).

Tender annuals

Originating in tropical and sub-tropical climates, tender annuals must be raised under heat in a greenhouse to flower within a year. If sown in the open soil after the danger of frosts have passed, they will not have a long enough season to mature and flower before the autumn frosts. The castor-oil plant (*Ricinus*) is a good example.

This drift of the annual *Cleome hassleriana* 'Pink Queen' combines well with perennials in a mixed border. The effect of the foliage of these plants is nearly as striking as that of the flowers.

What is a Biennial?

True annuals have a life-span of less than 12 months, and always flower within this time span. On the other hand, there are also biennials which take longer to flower. Biennials germinate in the first year, overwinter as a rosette of leaves and then flower during the following spring or summer. Occasionally biennials may be slow growing in their first year. If this is the case, the flowers may take an extra year to appear, blooming only in their third year.

Typical Biennial

The well-known foxglove, *Digitalis purpurea*, is a typical biennial. It is sown in the spring of the first year, either in trays or directly into the ground, and then it quickly germinates. Foxgloves grow on throughout the year with their basal leaves reaching almost full size before the start of the winter. They are fully hardy and need no winter protection. As spring of the second year approaches foxgloves grow rapidly, forming the familiar tall flower spike, which by early summer forms a statuesque spire of flowers.

Self-sowing

If left after flowering, foxgloves will produce copious amounts of seed which self-sow to produce another crop of plants. There are quite a number of biennials that behave in this way, which can save the gardener a lot of time. All that is required is to remove any excess or unwanted plants as well as any that have sown themselves in the wrong place.

Some plants often skip a year, the seed lying dormant then germinating the following year. *Delphinium staphisagria* and the Scotch thistle (*Onopordum acanthium*) often behave like this, but after a few years there

Biennials, such as this foxglove, *Digitalis purpurea*, usually form a rosette during their first year. After overwintering, they grow during the next spring to flower in the summer.

Lunaria annua is, in spite of its name, a biennial. Also known as honesty, its delicate silvery seed cases are very valuable in dried flower arrangements and decorations.

is enough residual seed in the soil for at least some to germinate every year giving a succession of flowers annually.

Direct Sowing

Many biennials and some short-lived perennials that are treated as biennials, such as wallflowers (*Erysimum*) and sweet William (*Dianthus barbatus*), are sown directly into the soil. They can also be sown in trays but do better in the ground. They should be sown in shallow drills in the late spring and thinned out when they have germinated. They are left in the rows until the autumn, when they will be big enough for transferring to their final flowering positions, which will often be an area of border that has just been cleared of the current year's annuals after the flowers have faded.

What is a Tender Perennial?

Gardeners are often unaware that many of the "annuals" they grow every year are, in fact, perennials, which in their wild state will go on flowering year after year. There are two reasons why these plants are treated as annuals in temperate regions. Some are short-lived while others are tender and would not survive a frosty winter. With care, both types could be treated as perennials, but their natures are such that it is advisable to discard the plants at the end of the year and then start afresh the following year.

Dahlias are an ideal choice for bringing the summer to a colourful end. However, dahlias are frost tender and must be lifted and stored in a frost-free place, such as a greenhouse or conservatory, before the weather turns cold. This striking, rich pink variety is 'Decorative'.

Short-lived perennials

These can be typified by wallflowers (*Erysimum*), snapdragons (*Antirrhinum*) and sweet Williams (*Dianthus barbatus*). Traditionally, these are sown afresh each year for flowering the next. However, if they are grown in soil that does not become too water-logged, and are trimmed back after flowering, they will flower again the following year, and even the next. With each year the flowering becomes a little less successful, so to get the best show it is best to treat them as an annual or biennial and sow each year.

Being perennial, these plants can also be propagated vegetatively. If the sown seed produces a wallflower that has an interesting colouring, it is possible to ensure that you have it again the next year by taking cuttings from non-flowering stems. Treat these as ordinary cuttings, simply potting them up when they have rooted, then planting them out in the autumn for flowering the following year.

Tender perennials

Different types of tender perennials can be treated in various ways by gardeners. Some, including petunias, are grown exactly like annuals, which means that they are sown every year and discarded after flowering. Another group, which includes pelargoniums and fuchsias, can be propagated by cuttings in the autumn, overwintered in a greenhouse or on a windowsill, and then planted out the following spring, once the danger of frosts has passed. A third group includes dahlias and tuberous begonias, and these have tubers which are simply lifted, stored in a frost-free place over the winter, and then planted out in the spring.

Several salvias, including this *Salvia sclarea*, are popular 'annuals', but they are actually perennials and can be overwintered in warmer areas.

Begonia semperflorens will flower non-stop from early summer through to the end of autumn when it will be killed by the first frosts if it is not moved inside.

Informal Schemes

One of the most common ways of using bedding plants is to plant them in an informal way. Whether roughly grouped or arranged in some loose pattern, they are planted in a glorious mixture that is rather reminiscent of old cottage gardens. While the longer-lasting bedding plants can produce a lovely display, and are invaluable for those with limited time, you can create even more interesting effects by using some of the more unusual annuals with relatively short flowering periods, thus changing the picture as the season progresses.

Design with care

Mixing plants without any real thought to their placement may well produce a riot of colour, but it can equally produce a chaotic mess. Most gardeners have probably come across examples of front gardens covered in a garish mixture of red, white, blue and orange all stirred up leaving an uncomfortable spectacle on which there is no place for the eye to rest. Take care when mixing the colours in beds and borders and try not to make the effect look too random and unplanned. Make the colours blend, the soft colours creating a restful scene, the brighter ones livening up the overall picture.

Seasonal annuals

In an informal setting, rather than the more typical bedding plants, less garish plants can often be used to create a bed that has more lasting interest. In spring, the soft colours of forget-me-nots (*Myosotis*), with foxgloves (*Digitalis*) pushing up through them and starting to flower before the forget-me-nots are over, are delightful. These can be followed by nigellas growing around the foxgloves which in turn can be

Cottage-garden informality has been created with seemingly random, yet not untidy, planting to achieve a really charming effect.

Here, a semi-formal scheme dominated by annuals is planted in blocks, bordered with *Limnanthes douglasii*, the poached egg plant.

replaced by stately mulleins (*Verbascum*). Later in the season both the yellow Mexican poppy (*Argemone mexicana*) and the white (*A. grandiflora*) might add their own charm. *Crepis rubra*, a short-lived perennial, and *Silene pendula* can be used to add a soft pink note to the planting. Pale cream could also

perhaps be introduced by planting *Collomia grandiflora*.

All these mixed colours will vary from week to week, creating a constantly changing soft, misty background against which splashes of eye-catching colour – perhaps the bright red of field poppies (*Papaver rhoeas*) – can be added to liven it up.

This wonderful haze of colour typifies a cottage garden. It may look totally random and unplanned but a certain degree of clever control has been exercised. Planning has ensured a good spread of colour and height, and a balance of flowers and foliage. Dense planting have made the border low-maintenance, as weeds are not able to prosper.

Formal Patterns

Patterns have always played an important part in garden design, especially in the larger gardens where there was space to lay things out on a grand scale. The grand designs are now seen only in municipal plantings, especially on the coast and in parks and other public spaces. For many years they have languished, but now a new generation of gardeners has produced a revival with some very imaginative plantings. There is no reason why the gardener with only a small plot should not produce scaled-down versions of these.

Straight lines and squiggles

All types of patterns can be used as long as they are not so intricate that the detail is lost as the plants grow. The plot to be planted can be divided up into geometrical shapes, such as straight lines, squares, rectangles, triangles, circles and so on. An alternative is to use free-form lines and shapes that interlock or at least react with one another to produce a pleasing pattern. Scrolls and teardrops might be two examples. Each of the lines or shapes can be delineated or filled in with a

With plenty of space to play with, creating a scheme like this is very gratifying. However, with a little ingenuity and good planning, there is no reason why such a scheme cannot be incorporated into a much smaller garden.

different colour of flower or leaf. It is worth remembering that foliage adds a great deal to these schemes.

Pictures

For those who want to do something special, creating a picture with flowers and foliage can be quite a challenge, and can be stunning when carried out well. At a municipal park level, one often sees the town's coat of arms (emblem) picked out in plants. Another popular theme is to make a working clock from flowers and foliage, with only the hands being made of metal or plastic. These types of designs are not only complicated and challenging but need a great deal of attention, especially with clipping, to keep them from going ragged and losing their image.

From paper to the bed

Patterns, especially intricate ones, need a great deal of planning and thought. They should be worked out

on graph paper in the same way that you might work out an embroidery or tapestry. You should then stretch a grid, using string and canes, across the plot to be planted, corresponding to the grid on the drawing. Using the string grid as a guide to position, you can then transfer the design to the ground by outlining the shapes with sand poured from a bottle.

Annuals arranged in simple geometric shapes create a satisfying rhythm along this long border. Blocks of single colours are easier on the eye than random mixes.

Bedding laid out in lines (straight or curved) with a regular repeat of certain plants or colours is one way to add formality to a bed or a whole garden.

Carpet Schemes

A long-standing tradition in public parks and gardens, carpet schemes can be used in a variety of ways. You can create intricate, formal designs, as demonstrated here, or you can use blocks of colour in bold, simple shapes, or a more informal, irregular scheme. The blocks can be created by planting out bedding plants, or you can sow directly into the soil, broadcasting different seed over each area. Striking colour contrasts can be achieved with flowers, or an interesting effect can be produced using only foliage plants. Many gardeners are under the impression that they do not have enough space for a carpet scheme, but if only small, low-growing plants are used, a very impressive design can be created in a relatively small area.

Pure blocks

Carpet bedding can be arranged in some form of pattern, possibly using an edging plant in a contrasting or sympathetic colour. The blocks can be regular in shape for a formal effect or they can be more random in appearance, perhaps with their edges in a series of curves if you want to achieve a more informal look.

The edges of a block are usually clear-cut, one type of plant ends and another starts, but there is no reason why they should not merge, especially if the colours blend well. The blocks can consist purely of one colour, bright red salvias for example, or they can be a subtle or contrasting mixture. Soft blue forget-me-nots (Myosotis) and pink tulips may be an unoriginal combination but it is nonetheless a very effective one. If you need inspiration for devising carpet bedding schemes, look at your local park or public gardens where they are common.

PLANTING A CARPET BEDDING SCHEME

1 Plan the scheme and draw it on graph paper. To transfer the design to the ground, first mark out a grid using canes and string, then draw out the design using distinctively coloured sand or compost (soil mix), poured from a container. If you are using plants to mark out the design, plant these first, along the lines of sand or compost (soil mix). Complete the planting by filling in between the lines with plants, following your plan. To avoid treading on the plants as you work, use a platform. Here, ladders supported on bricks, with timber planks placed along the rungs, have been used.

2 The finished scheme illustrates the benefit of patient work. Maintenance can be carried out using the same bridging technique as was used for its construction. Maintenance consists of removing any weeds and cutting back any growth that gets too long.

Working in three dimensions

It is worth remembering at the planning stage that different plants grow to different heights and spread, and you must make allowances for this. Otherwise your design may look ragged. Also, it may be possible to use the different heights to advantage to create a three-dimensional bed where some areas, or even certain plants, are higher than others.

Planning

It can be fun to work out different designs for carpet bedding schemes. For a formal scheme, you will need to draw the design on graph paper and mark out the grid on the ground using canes and string. Then draw the outline of the design on the ground by pouring sand from a bottle. For a less formal scheme, you can draw the design freehand on the ground with sand.

Parterres

Gardeners with space to spare can create a superior bedding scheme by planting a parterre and filling it with annuals. Parterres are patterns, either geometric or free-flowing, where each element is outlined by a low hedge. Where there is enough space, patterns can become very intricate and are often best viewed from above, perhaps from the top floor of the house. However, it is possible to create a small parterre in a relatively small garden. Indeed, the simplicity of such a garden and the relatively low maintenance it requires makes parterre ideal for this situation.

Hedges

The only real disadvantage of this type of scheme is that you have to wait several years for the hedges to grow to the required dimensions. The best plant to use is undoubtedly box (*Buxus sempervirens*), which is, unfortunately, very slow growing. This is an advantage in that it only needs cutting once or perhaps twice a year, but it does take some years to mature. A more rapid design can be achieved by using *Teucrium chamaedrys* or the grey-leaved *Santolina pinnata neapolitana*, but both need trimming a little more frequently than box. Lavender (*Lavandula*) is more untidy but makes a very colourful and fragrant parterre.

The hedges should be about 25cm (10in) high. Prepare the ground well and be certain to remove any perennial weeds or these will cause a problem later on. Dig in plenty of good organic material, as the hedge is likely to be there for many years and the better the condition of the soil, the better your hedge's condition, especially during a drought.

The infill

Make the most of the parterre and fill it with winter bedding plants as well as using it to create a colourful summer effect. Pansies are ideal for winter use. For spring, use forget-me-nots, primulas and wallflowers (*Erysimum*) as well as bulbs like tulips and narcissus.

For summer the choice is enormous. Each section of the parterre can show a different colour, or colours can be mixed. Traditional bedding plants that have a regularity in height and spread, a long flowering period and require little attention also make ideal candidates. Remember that foliage plants are excellent fillers – colourful Coleus (syn. *Solenostemon*), for example, or the subtly beautiful *Helichrysum petiolare*.

Permanence

Since the hedges take a while to grow, the basic shapes in the parterre cannot be changed each year. This makes annuals an ideal choice for filling the beds – they will not only vary from season to season but can be completely changed from year to year.

Wallflowers (*Erysimum*) are superb plants for creating mass planting within a parterre. The single colour establishes a striking effect, rather than the uneven one that mixing colours can often create.

Complicated patterns, like this one, look at their best with simple planting. Here, the parterre is filled with crimson, pink and white *begonia semperflorens* in effective blocks of colour.

Mixed Borders

Annual plants do not have to be used exclusively on their own in borders or beds devoted to various types of bedding scheme. They can be mixed with other plants, perennials and shrubs. This has the advantage of vastly increasing the variety of plants that can be used in the border (enlarging the gardener's palette, in other words), as well as allowing the introduction of a variable element into what is otherwise a fixed planting. A perennial border will vary slightly each year as the influence of the seasons and weather alters timing and the amount of flowering, but generally this type of border will remain much the same in appearance. By using different annuals, perhaps using reds instead of blues, the overall effect can be subtly altered.

Choosing Plants

Many of the popular bedding plants, such as red pelargoniums, are too rigid for the mixed border. It is better if possible to use annuals that look at home among herbaceous plants in a perennial or mixed border. Foxgloves (*Digitalis*) are ideal for early summer, and the opium poppy (*Papaver somniferum*) for later in the season. Both work well in a cottage-garden border. A more modern border with subtle colourings might include purple-leaved red orach (*Atriplex hortensis* 'Rubra') or soft blue love-in-a-mist (*Nigella damascena*). Foliage plants like *Helichrysum petiolare* add colour or act as linking themes between colours.

Perennial annuals

Some annuals self-sow regularly, reappearing every year without the gardener having to bother about sowing or planting them. These

PLANTING IN A MIXED BORDER

1 Remove any old plants and weeds from the area. Dig over the soil, avoiding disturbing the roots of nearby plants, and add well-rotted organic material if the soil has not been rejuvenated recently. If necessary, only dig the centre of the patch, where the plants will actually be positioned; their foliage will spread to fill the gap.

3 If you want to sow a drift of annuals, scatter the seed evenly over the ground. Rake in and water using a watering can fitted with a fine rose. If the ground is very dry, water and allow the water to drain away before sowing, then sow and water again. When the seedlings appear, thin them to the desired distance apart.

2 Feed the soil by scattering a slow-release general fertilizer, following the manufacturer's instructions. Work the fertilizer into the soil using a rake. If you are going to sow seed, break the soil down to a fine tilth at the same time. For bedding plants, the soil need not be as fine – an attractive, even tilth is sufficient.

4 If you wish to use bedding plants to fill the gap, simply plant them out at the appropriate intervals to the same depths they were in their pots. Gently firm in each plant, then rake the soil to even it and to remove any footprints. Water thoroughly.

work well in a mixed border where the seed can germinate and seedlings develop undisturbed, unlike in bedding areas where the soil is dug over every year and self-sowing plants can be a nuisance. Many self-seeding plants, such as borage (*Borago officinalis*), also associate well with a herbaceous border.

Planting

If the annual plants are to be dotted about the border, as foxgloves might be, they can be planted directly in

their positions. For a drift, however, or even a block of plants, it is preferable to dig over the area first and rejuvenate the soil with well rotted organic material.

When planting, avoid setting out the plants in straight rows. An uneven number of plants makes this easier; three or five making a more satisfactory arrangement than, say, two or four.

After the flowering period, simply remove the plants and begin to plan for next year.

How plants are named

All living things are classified according to a system based on principles that were devised by the 18th-century Swedish botanist, Carl Linnaeus. This system states that a particular plant genus (plural: genera) is a group of plants containing similar species. Beyond that there may be plants that are simply a slight variation of a species, or are a hybrid (cross) of different species or variations.

Scientific names

Under this system, plants have botanical names – often Latin but also derived from other languages – that consist of the genus name (for example, *Verbena*), followed by the name that denotes the particular species (for example, *hastata*). Some genera contain a huge number of species that may include annuals, perennials, shrubs and trees, while others contain just one species. Although all members of a genus are assumed to be related to each other, this is not always visually obvious. It is useful to keep in mind that a species is defined scientifically as individuals that are alike and tend naturally to breed with each other.

Despite this system, botanists and taxonomists (the experts who classify living things) often disagree about the basis on which a plant has been named. This is why it is useful for a plant to retain its synonym (abbreviated to syn. in the text), or alternative name. Incorrect names often gain widespread usage, and in some cases, two plants thought to have separate identities, and with two different names, are found to be the same plant.

A well-known example of naming confusion is the genus *Pelargonium*. Until the 19th century, pelargonium plants were included in the genus *Geranium*, and despite being classified separately for over a century, they are still popularly known as geraniums.

Variations on a theme

Genetically, many plants are able to change over time to adapt to a changing environment. In the wild, individuals within a species that are not well adapted will not survive, so all survivors will look the same. The average garden is a more controlled environment, so gardeners can choose to encourage and grow on variations within a species that have small but

This is *Centaurea hypoleuca* 'John Coutts'. John Coutts is the name that has been given to a dark pink form of the pink knapweed species, *Centaurea hypoleuca*.

pleasing differences such as variegated leaves and double flowers. The terms for these variations are subspecies (abbreviated to subsp.), variety (var.), form (f., similar to variety and often used interchangeably) and cultivar. A cultivar is a variation that would not occur in the wild but has been produced and maintained solely by cultivation. Variations are given names in single quotes, for example *Papaver orientale* 'Allegro'.

Hybrids

When plant species breed with each other, the result is a hybrid. Rare in the wild, crossing is very common among plant-breeders, done specially in order to produce plants with desirable qualities such as larger or double blooms, variegated foliage and greater frost resistance. A multiplication sign (x) is used to indicate a hybrid, and the name often gives a clear idea of the hybrid's origins.

Plant Groups

A Group of plants is a group of very similar variations. Their names do not have quotation marks around them – for example *Lobularia martima* Easter Bonnet Series.

The geranium is a well-known case of naming confusion, as many plants that actually belong to the genus *Pelargonium* are very commonly referred to as geraniums.

How to use the directory

Within the directory, plants are arranged alphabetically, by genus. Each main entry features a general introduction to that genus, plus specific useful information such as tips on propagation and which hardiness zone the genus belongs to. This is followed by a selection of plants from that genus, also arranged alphabetically according to their most widely accepted names. One of these entries might be a species, a hybrid (or group of hybrids), a variety, form or cultivar. Each is given a useful description that may include height and spread.

Caption
The full botanical name of the plant in question is given with each photograph.

Genus name
This is the internationally accepted botanical name for a group of related plant species.

Common name
This popular, non-scientific name applies to the whole of the plant genus.

How to obtain
This gives advice on getting hold of plants as seeds, plants or trays of plants.

Cultivation
This section gives the level of sun or shade that the plants described in the selection either require or tolerate, advice on the best type of soil in which they should be grown, and any other helpful tips that might be appropriate.

Propagation
This section gives essential information on how and when to increase the plant – from seed, by dividing plants or by taking various types of cutting. Many annuals entries also give the best temperature at which to propagate a plant, often with specific centigrade (and Fahrenheit) figures given.

Uses
If given, this section advises on how to get the best from a plant – using in borders or containers or to brighten up dark corners, for example.

Individual plant entry
This starts with the current botanical name of the plant in bold, and this can refer to a species, subspecies, hybrid, variant or cultivar. If a synonym (syn.) is given, this provides the synonym, or synonyms (alternative names) for a plant. A common name may be given after the botanical name.

Plant description
This gives a description of the plant, along with any other information that may be helpful and relevant.

Eccremocarpus scaber

ECCREMOCARPUS
Chilean glory flower

This is a small genus containing five species of perennial climbing plants of which one, *E. scaber*, is regularly seen in gardens. It is debatable whether this should be classified in gardening terms as a perennial or as an annual since it is regularly treated as both. However, the majority of gardeners use it as an annual climber. It is fast growing and so well suited for use as an annual. It will grow up through other plants or up twiggy supports up to 5m (15ft) if used as a perennial. As an annual it reaches 2–3m (6–10ft).

How to obtain Chilean glory flowers are occasionally seen in pots but they are more frequently sold as seed. Most seed merchants carry them.

Cultivation These plants will grow well in a reasonably fertile, well-drained soil. A sunny position is needed. If they are planted against a warm wall, the plants may overwinter and produce flowers for a second year. Z9.

Propagation Sow seed in early spring under glass at 13–16°C (55–60°F).

Uses Grow as a climbing plant either in borders or against walls or fences. Chilean glory flowers can also be grown in large containers if supported by a wigwam of sticks or a framework.

Eccremocarpus scaber
This is the main species grown, which has orange or flame-red tubular flower heads.

Photograph
Each entry features a full-colour photograph that makes identification easy.

Genus introduction
This provides a general introduction to the genus and may state the number of species within that genus. Other information featured here may include general advice on usage, preferred conditions, and plant-care, as well as subspecies, hybrids (indicated by an x symbol in the name), varieties and cultivars (featuring names in single quotes) that are available.

Size information
The average expected height and spread of a genus or individual plant is frequently given, although growth rates may vary depending on location and conditions. Metric measurements always precede imperial ones. Average heights and spreads are given (as H and S) wherever possible and appropriate, and more consistently for perennials, although it must be noted that dimensions can vary a great deal.

Plant hardiness zone
A plant hardiness zone is given at the end of this section. Zones give a general indication of the average annual minimum temperature for a particular geographical area. The smaller number indicates the northernmost zone it can survive in and the higher number the southernmost zone that the plant will tolerate. In most cases, only one zone is given. (See page 96 for details of zones and a zone map.)

Additional information

Other plants
If given, these sections provide brief information about common types that are available and other recommended (often rarer) plants to look out for.

A directory of annuals

This directory offers a comprehensive array of annual plants – all the familiar favourites plus some rarer specimens – among which gardeners of all levels will find ample choice to help them make the most of their garden space.

The initial introduction for each entry is either for the whole genus or the main species grown. Beyond this the entry is split between more common species and cultivars and those which are less common. The advent of the internet has meant that it is often possible to obtain seed, including that of very rare plants, from around the world. Growing rarer species can be rewarding as they are often particularly beautiful. On the other hand they may be less common because they are more difficult to grow and thus create a challenge. If no temperatures are given, seed can be germinated in a cool greenhouse or even in pots left outside.

Where seed is listed as being available from seed merchants, this can be purchased directly from the merchants using their catalogues or from a store or garden centre. Some unusual varieties are available mail order only from a catalogue. Many specialist societies make seed available to their members – a good way of obtaining rarer seed. Check catalogues carefully as some seed merchants have idiosyncratic or very out-of-date ways of naming plants that may be at variance with botanical names and with those that have been used in this book.

Begonia semperflorens has long been a very popular gardener's choice and offers a wide selection of attractively coloured cultivars.

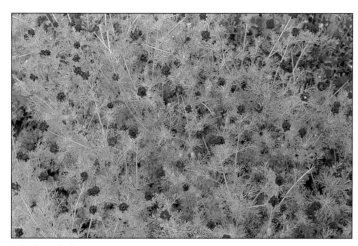

Adonis aestivalis

ADONIS
Pheasant's Eye

This is a genus containing about 20 species of annuals and perennials. Of these, only a couple of the annuals are generally grown. These are so similar that the gardener might not notice the slight botanical difference. They are thin and upright plants with feathery foliage. The flowers are bright red and cup-shaped; they look like the red buttercups to which they are related. These plants thrive in disturbed ground; they were once widespread among crops in cornfields but they are rarely seen growing wild today. They are attractive enough to be used in borders, particularly when planted in large drifts, but they are more commonly seen in beds devoted to wild flowers. They are hardy. H 45cm (18in) S 15cm (6in).

How to obtain These plants can generally only be obtained as seed. This is widely available from good seed merchants as well as from specialist societies.

Cultivation Thin the plants to about 15cm (6in) to produce a dense mass. They need a soil enriched with plenty of well-rotted organic material. It should be free draining. A position in full sun is needed. Z6.

Propagation Sow directly into the soil where the plants are to grow in either autumn or in spring. An autumn sowing produces more vigorous plants.

Uses Adonis look good in mixed beds and borders, especially in wild-flower gardens.

Adonis aestivalis

This is the most commonly seen plant. It has very finely cut leaves which set off the bright crimson flowers with a darker centre. These are produced over a very long period from midsummer to well into autumn. If you can find it there is a rare variety of *A. aestivalis* called *citrina* which has yellow flowers.

Adonis annua

This plant is very similar to the previous species but the flowers are a deeper red.

Other plants There is also a species called *A. flammea* which is worth seeking out. It is similar to the ones described above except that the flowers are larger.

AGERATUM
Floss flower

This moderately large genus contains about 40 species of perennials and shrubs as well as annuals. There is only one annual that is in general cultivation, namely *A. houstonianum*, but fortunately it has plenty of cultivars so the gardener does not lack choice. The plants are rounded and produce fluffy sprays of blue flowers. Over the years pink and white cultivars have also been introduced. Ageratum have long been used as bedding plants, and are often grown in swathes in a bed or as ribbon-like edging along a path or around beds. H and S 20–30cm (8–12in), athough some cultivars reach up to 75cm (30in).

How to obtain Ageratums can be bought as seed from most seed merchants and they are available as young plants in spring from garden centres and nurseries. Plants may be sold as "Ageratum" without any cultivar being given.

Cultivation Plant out after frosts have passed in a fertile soil in full sun. Z10.

Propagation Seed can be sown under glass at 16–18°C (60–64°F) in spring. For larger plants sow in late autumn and overwinter the resulting plants in warm conditions.

Uses Ageratums make excellent bedding plants, grown in blocks or lines. They are good in window boxes and other containers. Some are good for cutting.

Ageratum houstonianum 'Bavaria'
This pretty cultivar has fluffy flower heads in blue and white. H up to 25cm (10in).

Ageratum houstonianum 'Blue Danube'
This is a short form which produces attractive pale blue flowers. H 20cm (8in).

Ageratum houstonianum 'Blue Horizon'
This is a tall variety with purple-blue clusters of flowers, which is good for cutting. H 45–60cm (18–24in) or more.

Ageratum houstonianum Hawaii Series
These short plants produce flowers either in a mixture of colours ('Hawaii Mixed', 'Hawaii Garland') or in individual colours such as 'Hawaii White'. H 15cm (6in).

Ageratum houstonianum 'Swing Pink'
This is another dwarf form, which produces pretty pink flowers. H 15cm (6in).

Ageratum houstonianum 'Purple Fields'
The flowers of this cultivar are purple. H 25cm (10in).

Ageratum houstonianum 'Red Sea'
Bright red buds open to purple-red flowers. They are good for cutting. H 45cm (18in).

Ageratum houstonianum

Agrostemma githago 'Milas'

AGROSTEMMA
Corn cockle

This is a small genus of annuals of which only a couple are generally cultivated. They grow naturally on disturbed or waste ground, and as their name implies they were once often seen growing in fields of corn.

Corn cockles are tall plants which have thin, wiry stems and open funnel-shaped flowers. These are purple with a white centre, and appear in summer. Although they work well in drifts in a mixed border they are often grown in wild-flower gardens. H 1m (3ft) in good conditions, S 30cm (12in).

How to obtain Corn cockle is usually available as seed from seed merchants or from specialist societies. Plants are rarely offered for sale, but they can occasionally be found.

Cultivation Corn cockles grow in a fertile soil in a sunny position. Plants are shown at their best when they are tightly planted together, so do not thin too vigorously. They need support in exposed positions. Z8

Propagation Sow the seed in spring where the plants are to grow. If left to set seed, corn cockles will usually self-sow.

Uses Corn cockles are best grown in either mixed borders or a wild area of the garden.

Agrostemma githago and *A. gracilis*

These species are similar to each other, and produce the purple flowers described above. The seed of *A. githago* is more common, and there are some cultivars.

Agrostemma githago 'Milas'

This is the cultivar most widely grown. It has pinker flowers than the species.

Agrostemma githago 'Milas Cerise'

This is very similar to the previous cultivar, except that the flowers are cerise.

Agrostemma githago 'Ocean Pearl'

This is a beautiful cultivar with pure white flowers. It is a must for the white garden.

ALCEA
Hollyhock

This genus produces the much-loved hollyhock. This is *A. rosea*, a perennial that is now generally grown as a biennial. Hollyhocks are very tall plants, but there are shorter cultivars that are more suitable for smaller gardens. They have one or more tall stems on which appear open funnel-shaped flowers. Some cultivars have double flowers. The flowers are produced over most of the summer and into autumn. The plants are hardy. H 2.5m (8ft).

How to obtain Hollyhocks can be purchased as seed from seed merchants or as plants from garden centres and nurseries. The plants may be sold simply as "Hollyhocks" with no colour given. The seed can be mixed or one colour. *Alcea* may be listed as its former name *Althaea*.

Cultivation Plant or thin out seedlings to intervals of 60cm (24in). They like a deep, rich soil that is well-drained. Plants may need staking in exposed areas. Hollyhocks can suffer from rust so remove them after flowering and raise new plants from seed rather than keeping old ones for subsequent years. Z4.

Propagation Sow seed where the plants are to grow. Plants left to seed will self-sow.

Uses Hollyhocks are excellent plants for either mixed or herbaceous borders.

Alcea rosea 'Black Beauty'

As its name suggests this is a black-flowered variety.

Alcea rosea 'Chater's Double'

This cultivar produces fully double flowers that look like pompoms. They come in a wide range of colours. The seed is sold as mixed or individual colours.

Alcea rosea 'Majorette Mixed'

This cultivar produces semi-double blooms in mixed pastel shades. H 1m (3ft).

Alcea rosea 'Chater's Double'

Alcea rosea 'Nigra'

This is an ancient cultivar known for at least 400 years. It carries very dark red flowers that are almost black. There is a rarer double form of the same colour, called 'Nigra Plena'.

Alcea rosea 'Peaches 'n' Dreams'

This plant produces very frilly double flowers in a soft peach-pink colour.

Alcea rosea 'Zanzibar'

Flowers in a range of pastel shades are produced on tall plants. H 2m (6ft).

Other plants *Alcea ficifolia* is another hollyhock treated as a biennial. It is similar to the above except that the leaves are more lobed. The flowers are yellow or orange, single or double. 'Antwerp Mixed' is a mix of pastel shades.

Alcea rosea

Tall annuals

Agrostemma githago 'Milas'	Helianthus annuus
Alcea rosea	Lavatera trimestris
Amaranthus caudatus	Moluccella laevis
Centaurea americana	Nicotiana affinis
Cleome spinosa	Nicotiana sylvestris
Consolida ambigua	Oenothera biennis
Cosmos	Ricinus communis
Dahlia	Tithonia rotundifolia
Datura	Zea mays
Gilia rubra	Zinnia

Amaranthus caudatus

Anchusa capensis 'Dawn Mixed'

AMARANTHUS
Love-lies-bleeding

A large genus of half-hardy annuals and short-lived perennials. *A. caudatus* is of most interest to the general gardener. It has dangling flowers that look like bunches of lambs' tails or ropes, mainly in crimson or purple. They have an old-fashioned look about them and are not seen as often in gardens as they once were. They can be used in small groups in general borders or in bedding schemes. They are long flowering through summer and autumn.
How to obtain The main way to acquire these is as seed from merchants. Occasionally plants are available from garden centres.
Cultivation Plant out after the threat of frosts has passed in a soil with plenty of well-rotted organic material. It should be moisture-retentive but free-draining. Z5.
Propagation Sow the seed under glass in the spring at 16–18°C (60–64°F).
Uses These plants are best grown in general mixed borders or in bedding schemes.

Amaranthus caudatus
This, the main species grown, can reach 1.2m (4ft), but is often less. S 60cm (24in). The tassels are red or purple, although there is a cultivar 'Viridis' or 'Green Tails' with greenish flowers.

Amaranthus cruentus
Known as Prince's Feather, this plant has more upright spikes in a variety of reds and yellows.

There are a large number of cultivars available, including 'Red Cathedral' which has attractive scarlet foliage.

Amaranthus hypochondriacus
Upright spikes of flowers, mainly in shades of red. 'Green Thumb' has green flowers and 'Pygmy Torch' is a dwarf variety only 45cm (18in) high.

Amaranthus tricolor
This is Chinese spinach, grown for its decorative foliage which comes in several colours. 'Joseph's Coat' has a mixture of red, yellow, brown and green leaves, while 'Illumination' has bright pinkish-red, gold and brown leaves.

ANCHUSA
Anchusa

This is a genus of about 35 species of which a number are annuals or biennials. One in particular is of interest to the annual gardener, namely *A. capensis*. This is strictly speaking a perennial but it is usually grown as an annual. It is a clump-forming plant with long, narrow leaves that are rough with bristles, and sprays of shallow funnel-shaped flowers that flower in summer. The flowers are generally blue with a white throat although there are other cultivars with a range of colours. H up to 45cm (18in) S 20cm (8in).
How to obtain These plants are available as seed from seed merchants and specialist societies.
Cultivation Plant out or thin the young plants at 30cm (12in) intervals. Any reasonable garden soil will do but a well-draining, moisture-retentive one is preferred. Plant in full sun. Z9.
Propagation When treated as an annual, sow the seed under glass in early spring at 16–18°C (60–64°F). It can be treated as a biennial by sowing outside in summer and transplanting in the autumn or spring.
Uses Anchusas can be used as bedding plants or grown in a mixed border.

Anchusa capensis
The species is less popular than in the past, but it is still an excellent blue-flowered plant.

Anchusa capensis 'Blue Angel'
This is an attractive cultivar which produces flowers that are bright blue in colour.

Anchusa capensis 'Blue Bird'.
Indigo-blue flowers. This is an old variety but it is probably still the most popular.

Anchusa capensis 'Dawn Mixed'
The flowers are in a mixture of colours – mainly blue with white, pink, red and purple.

Anchusa capensis 'Dwarf Mix'
These plants are smaller and more compact with blue flowers. The seed is more difficult to find.

Anchusa capensis 'Pink Bird'
As its name suggests, this cultivar has pink flowers.

ANGELICA
Angelica

This genus of about 50 species is known mainly to gardeners for the herb *A. archangelica*. However, there is a species that has only recently entered general

Anchusa capensis

Angelica gigas

cultivation that makes an excellent biennial for the border. This is *A. gigas*, a native of Japan. It has gorgeous heads of maroon flowers which are perfect for the mixed border, or for the edge of a woodland or shrub bed. It can be dramatic and eyecatching. The plants are monocarpic, that is they may grow for one, two or more years before they flower, but once they have flowered they die. Fortunately angelicas make good foliage plants so their growing time is not wasted. H 2m (6ft) S 1–1.2m (3–4ft). They are completely hardy.

How to obtain The seed is available from some seed merchants. The plants are available from nurseries and some garden centres.

Cultivation Any reasonable garden soil will do, but the richer and more moist the soil, the more splendid the plants will be. Plant out as soon as possible in either spring or autumn, in either full sun or partial shade. Z4.

Propagation Angelicas are grown from seed which is sown in autumn or spring.

Uses Angelicas look very good in borders or in woodland settings. They are excellent for wilder, more exotic plantings.

Angelica gigas

This is a truly splendid towering plant. The flowers are carried in domed heads produced on black stems above dissected, bright green leaves. The large heads are a fabulous dark crimson in colour. H 2m (6ft) S 1–1.2m (3–4ft).

Antirrhinum 'Coronette Bronze'

Antirrhinum 'Coronette White'

Other plants *Angelica archangelica* is mainly grown as a herb but it is decorative enough to deserve a place in the border, especially in a wild-flower garden. The flowers are white, and the stems and leaves dullish green. *Angelica atropurpurea* is similar to the previous plant, also having white flowers, but the stems are a contrasting purple. You will have to hunt a little further to find the seed and plants.

ANTIRRHINUM
Snapdragon

Surely all gardeners know these excellent garden plants. Quite a number of the 40 species are in cultivation but most gardeners grow just *A. majus*, which is the common snapdragon. These are bushy plants producing several spikes of curiously shaped flowers. Plants are now available in a wide range of colours and sizes. There are some forms with double flowers and others with variegated foliage. One impressive breakthrough is the trailing varieties, which look wonderful in hanging baskets. H 25–60cm (10–24in) S 45cm (18in).

How to obtain All seed merchants offer several varieties and plants can be bought from garden centres, both as colour mixtures or separate colours. The plants are available either in trays or individual pots.

Cultivation Antirrhinums will grow in any good garden soil. Plant or thin to about 45cm (18in). Z7.

Propagation Grow from seed sown under glass at 16–18°C (60–64°F) in early spring. The seed can also be sown in open ground in spring for late-flowering plants.

Uses Antirrhinums are excellent for mixed borders or for bedding. They are also very good plants for children's gardens. Some varieties are suitable for containers including hanging baskets. Taller varieties make good cut flowers

Antirrhinum majus 'Chinese Lanterns'

This is one of the new trailing forms. It produces flowers in a mixture of colours.

Antirrhinum majus Coronette Series

This attractive plant series carries flowers in a mix of colours. They are also available as individual

colours, as in the cultivars 'Coronette Bronze' and 'Coronette White'. H 60cm (24in).

Antirrhinum majus 'Floral Showers'

A dwarf collection, with plants growing up to 20cm (8in) tall.

Antirrhinum majus Mme Butterfly Series

These plants produce double flowers in a mixture of colours. H 75cm (30in).

Antirrhinum majus Rocket Series

As its name suggests, this is a very tall range. Plants reach up to 1.2m (4ft) in good conditions.

Other plants These include 'Sonnet Light Rose' and 'Black Prince'. Check seed catalogues for a better idea of the complete range.

Antirrhinum majus 'Black Prince'

Antirrhinum 'Sonnet Light Rose'

Arctotis 'Flame'

ARCTOTIS
African daisy

This is a genus of some 50 species from South Africa. There are several annual and short-lived perennials that are used as bedding plants. They are rather splendid daisies, generally having white or orange petals with a dark ring round the central black or brown disc. They are bright and gay but have the disadvantage that they shut up if the sun is not shining and generally shut half-way through the afternoon. However, the flowers of some newer cultivars stay open longer. H 60cm (24in) S 30cm (12in).
How to obtain The best way is to obtain these plants as seed since the main seed merchants sell them. They can also be bought as plants from many garden centres.

Arctotis × hybrida 'Apricot'

Cultivation A well-drained soil in full sun is essential. Plant out after frosts have passed. Z9.
Propagation Sow the seed in early spring under glass at 16–18°C (60–64°F) and prick out into individual pots.
Uses These make excellent bedding plants so long as they have plenty of sunshine. They are also good for very well-drained border, such as a gravel garden. They can be used as cut flowers.

Arctotis fastuosa
One of the easiest species to obtain. It has large 10cm (4in) flowers with orange petals and a black inner band. It provides one of the best-known cultivars, 'Zulu Prince', whose flowers have gleaming white petals with black and orange inner bands.

Arctotis Harlequin Hybrids
A mixed strain of seed with daisies in white, orange, pink, red or apricot. The Harlequin New Hybrids have the same range of colours and sometimes also have inner black bands. They also include some individual cultivars such as 'Apricot'.

Arctotis venusta
The flowers of this attractive plant are creamy-white in colour, with a blue central disc.

Other plants Arctotis hirsuta is a hairy plant, with orange, yellow or white flowers with a yellow inner band and a black central disc.

ARGEMONE
Prickly poppy
A genus of about 30 species of which there are a number of annuals in cultivation. The name prickly poppy refers to the fact that the large seed heads are covered in vicious spines, as are the leaves. Although this makes weeding and seed collecting a dangerous occupation, the flowers are absolutely delightful and so these plants are worth growing. The flowers, like many poppies, look like crumpled tissue paper. They are either glistening white or a wonderful yellow with a contrasting central boss of red stamens. The prickly leaves are an

Argemone grandiflora

attractive colour; a bluish-green with silvery markings. These are rather open, sprawling plants, so they are not suited to bedding schemes. They look good mixed with other plants in the front of a herbaceous border. Most are short-lived perennials and may last into a second year. The plants will flower all summer and continue into autumn if they are deadheaded regularly. They can reach up to 1.5m (5ft) but are usually no more than 45cm (18in) in most garden situations.
How to obtain The seed for prickly poppies can be obtained from some of the more specialized seed merchants as well as from specialist societies. The plants can occasionally be found in nurseries.
Cultivation Plant out after frosts have passed in a well-drained soil that is not too rich. Prickly poppies tolerate poor soils. Z8.
Propagation Sow seed at 16–18°C (60–64°F) under glass in the early spring.
Uses These plants are best used in a mixed border. They are excellent for gravel gardens.

Argemone mexicana

Argemone grandiflora
This has white or yellow flowers up to 10cm (4in) across. The leaves have white veining.

Argemone mexicana
This is very similar to the previous plant except that the flowers are slightly smaller and are generally yellow. There is a creamy-yellow variety *ochroleuca*, as well as the white forms 'Alba' or 'White Lustre' and a deeper, orange-yellow form 'Yellow Lustre'. These are more difficult to find than the species but they are worth looking out for.

Other plants A. pleiacantha has large white flowers up to 15cm (6in) across. Otherwise it is very similar to A. grandiflora. A. polyanthemos is not so prickly; the large flowers are either white or pale lilac.

ARGYRANTHEMUM
Argyranthemum
A genus of 23 species which were once classified as *Chrysanthemum* to which they have a great visual resemblance. They have daisy-like

Argemone platyceras 'Silver Charm'

Argyranthemum 'Jamaica Primrose'

flowers either with an outer ring of petals and a yellow central disc or an outer ring of petals with a similar coloured pompom of petals in the middle. The colours are white, yellow or pink. These flowers are produced over a long period, through the summer and up to the first frosts. They are tender perennials, which are usually treated as annuals. H 60–100cm (2–3ft) S 60cm (24in).
How to obtain Argyranthemums are usually purchased as plants in individual pots. They are available from garden centres and nurseries.
Cultivation Plant in a well-drained fertile soil after frosts are over. They need a sunny position. Z9.
Propagation Take basal cuttings from plants in spring or tip cuttings in summer; overwinter the resulting plants under glass.
Uses Argyranthemums are versatile plants that can be used in mixed borders, as bedding plants and in containers.

Argyranthemum 'Blizzard'
This cultivar produces double flowers which have narrow, shaggy white petals.

Argyranthemum 'Cornish Gold'
The flowers of this cultivar are yellow with yellow centres. H 60cm (24in).

Argyranthemum frutescens
This is one of the *Argyranthemum* species from which many of the cultivars are derived. It is also grown in its own right, and has yellow flowers.

Argyranthemum 'Jamaica Primrose'
One of the best, with soft primrose-yellow petals and a golden central disc.

Argyranthemum 'Mary Cheek'
Pink outer petals surround a pink pompom of petals. This is a smallish plant. H 45cm (18in).

Argyranthemum 'Vancouver'

Argyranthemum 'Mary Wootton'
This plant is similar to the previous one but it is much larger. H 1.2m (4ft).

Argyranthemum 'Petite Pink'
The flowers of these plants have pink outer petals and a yellow central disc. H 30cm (12in).

Argyranthemum 'Snowstorm'
Another short plant with white outer petals and a yellow central disc. H 30cm (12in).

Argyranthemum 'Vancouver'
This is a pink-flowered cultivar. which is similar to 'Mary Wootton'.

Other plants Argyranthemum gracile 'Chelsea Girl' is one of the finest cultivars to use in containers; it is often overwintered and grown as a standard. It is also used as a bedding plant. The flowers are white and the foliage is very fine and hair-like.

ATRIPLEX
Red orache
A large genus of plants that are mainly weeds or plants of no consequence. However, there is one that is important to gardeners, namely *A. hortensis*. This is often grown as a spinach substitute in the vegetable garden, but the red form 'Rubra' is widely grown as a very decorative plant. It is very tall and makes a positive statement in the border. H 1.5m (5ft) S 75cm (30in).
How to obtain Red orache is best grown from seed which is widely available. You occasionally see plants but they rarely grow to their full potential because they tend to be starved in small pots.

Cultivation Transplant any seedlings when they are very young or they will not thrive. Thin or transplant to 75cm (30in) intervals. Red oraches will grow in any garden soil but they do best in a rich, well-fed one. A sunny site is best; in shade the leaves turn green. Z6.
Propagation Sow the seed where the plants are to grow in autumn or in spring.
Uses These plants work well in mixed borders but they can also be used as a tall centrepiece in a bedding scheme.

Atriplex hortensis 'Rubra'
This is the most commonly grown plant. Its leaves, stems and spikes of small but numerous flowers are all a deep purplish-red. This colour looks rather leaden in dull light but it turns a fabulous blood-red against a setting sun. The young leaves are a colourful addition to salads. The plant self-sows madly, so cut it down before the seed is shed. H 1.5m (5ft) S 75cm (30in).

Other plants The Plume series is a newer strain of seed that includes 'Copper Plume', which has deep red flowers, 'Gold Plume' (straw-coloured flowers), 'Green Plume' (bright green flowers) and 'Red Plume' (deep, rich red flowers and foliage). These plants are rather more difficult to track down, but they are undoubtedly worth seeking out for their decorative quality.

Atriplex hortensis 'Rubra'

Long-flowering annuals

Ageratum	Nicotiana
Argyranthemum	Pelargonium
Begonia	Petunia
Brachyscome iberidifolia	Portulaca grandiflora
Calendula officinalis	Salvia
Heliotropium arborescens	Tagetes
Impatiens	Thunbergia alata
Lobelia erinus	Tropaeolum majus
Matthiola incana	Verbena × hybrida
Mimulus	Viola × wittrockiana

Barbarea vulgaris 'Variegata'

BARBAREA
Barbarea

This is a small genus of plants, most of which are of no interest to the gardener. The exception is *B. vulgaris* which is known as winter cress and commonly grown as a salad ingredient. This is of no consequence in the flower garden but it has a variegated form 'Variegata' that is widely grown as a foliage plant. The leaves are darkish green and are splashed with golden-yellow. It is a member of the cabbage family and the flowers are the familiar four-petalled yellow ones which add little to the border and so are usually removed. It is worth leaving some on the plant, however, so that you have seed for the following year. The plants are biennial. They are tall and narrow, so quite a number of plants are needed to make an impact. H 45cm (18in) when grown in good soil, S 20cm (8in) across.
How to obtain You can get barbareas as individual plants but this is an expensive way of buying them if you need a lot. You may have to search for seed but it is available from a number of seed merchants. Alternatively buy one plant and collect seed from it.
Cultivation Barbareas can be grown in any reasonable garden soil, and can be used either in a sunny or in a partially shaded position. Remove flowers unless seed is required. Z6.
Propagation Sow the seed in the open, as soon as possible after it has been collected.

Uses Barbareas look good in mixed borders or bedding schemes, and help brighten up darker corners.

BASSIA
Burning bush

A genus of about 25 species of perennials and annuals of which only one is grown in gardens. This is *B. scoparia* in the form *trichophylla*. It is a foliage plant that forms a bright green bush which is attractive in its own right. However, as the summer proceeds it turns a brilliant red or orange, hence its name "burning bush". The flowers are inconspicuous and of no relevance to most gardeners. Burning bushes are truly spectacular plants but while they used to be very popular but they are seen less frequently now. This is a pity since they make excellent plants for bedding as well as for filling gaps in perennial borders. Being green in the first instance they act as a foil for more brightly coloured plants. They look and feel soft.

Plants vary in size considerably depending on soil and other conditions. They can be anything from a modest 30cm (12in) up to 1.5m (5ft) when growing well. They are conical in shape and tend not to be so wide as they are tall. S up to 45cm (18in).
How to obtain Although it is now less frequently seen than in the past, seed is still available from many merchants. It is often listed under its old name *Kochia trichopylla*. It is also worth looking out for the plants in garden centres. Z6.

Begonia semperflorens (flower detail)

Cultivation Do not plant out until after the frosts have finished, then plant in any reasonably fertile soil in a sunny position. Larger plants need shelter from winds. Z6.
Propagation Sow under glass at 16–18°C (60–64°F) in early spring. It is also possible to sow seed directly where the plants are to grow in late spring, but the resulting bushes are not very big.
Uses Excellent for borders and bedding and are especially good as central features. They can be used as specimen plants in containers.

Other plants There are no cultivars. It would be a bonus if different coloured forms were to be bred.

BEGONIA
Begonia

This is a very large genus of some 900 species of which a number are in cultivation along with a great many cultivars. The begonia is a plant that gardeners can become very attached to, and many people collect different varieties. Here we can only scratch the surface of this fascinating group of plants, concentrating on those that are grown in the garden. (There are many more that are cultivated in greenhouses. These are in fact perennials but are treated as annuals since they are tender.) The most common garden form are the semperflorens begonias. Another group that are often seen growing outside, especially as container plants are the tuberhybrida begonias.
How to obtain The easiest way to obtain begonias is by buying plants, which are available from garden centres. Semperflorens can be bought in trays or pots and tuberhybrida in pots. Frequently they are sold as simply 'begonias' with no cultivar name given. Trays often contain plants in mixed

Bassia scoparia

Begonia semperflorens

colours, so you will need to buy plants in flower if you want particular forms. Both can also be obtained as seed. Gardeners who want to start a collection should go to specialist nurseries for a wider selection.

Cultivation Plant out after the last frosts in a good humus-rich soil which is either neutral or acid. Begonias need a lightly shaded position. Z10.

Propagation Sow seed in early spring under glass at about 20°C (68°F). Take cuttings in early summer and overwinter the young plants under warm glass.

Uses Semperflorens are superb in bedding schemes since they are usually of uniform height and so look good when planted in blocks. They are also used a lot in all forms of containers. The tuberhybrids can be used in bedding but they are shown at their best in containers.

Begonia semperflorens

These are low bushy plants with succulent stems and waxy-looking leaves and flowers. The flowers are commonly white, pink or red. They appear in early summer and continue until the first frosts. The foliage is either green or bronzy-purple. There are many cultivars to choose from. However for most garden purposes it is simply a matter of picking a colour that suits your scheme rather than seeking out any specific variety. H and S 15–45cm (6–18in).

Begonia × tuberhybrida

The tuberous begonias produce much more blowsy flowers. They are usually, but not always doubles in a wide variety of colours, often coming as picotees (edged in a different colour). These are generally too delicate for bedding, but they make good container plants. H 25–45cm (10–18in) S 30cm (12in).

BELLIS
Daisy

The humble common daisy may be the bane of gardeners' lawns but it is nevertheless a very pretty flower and there are some excellent varieties for use in borders and bedding. To many modern gardeners they look old-fashioned and have a quality reminiscent of cottage gardens. As a result, they are not seen quite so much nowadays as previously. There are about 15 species but it is the only the common daisy, *B. perennis* that is of interest. It has

Bellis perennis 'Rogli Rose'

given rise to a large number of garden varieties. The attraction of many of these is that their flowers are double. They are either white or shades of pink, sometimes both. Strictly speaking, these plants are perennials but they are usually treated as annuals because flower quality reduces in later years. H and S 20cm (8in).

How to obtain Daisies can be obtained in single pots and occasionally in trays. Some varieties are also available as seed.

Cultivation Daisies grow in any reasonable garden soil. They prefer a sunny position, but they will tolerate a little shade. Z4.

Propagation Divide existing plants in spring. Sow seed in the open ground in summer and transplant in the autumn or spring. They can also be sown in early spring under cool glass.

Uses Use in bedding schemes, along paths or border edges, or as clumps in a mixed border.

Bellis perennis

The common daisy is usually considered a weed but it can look attractive when grown in a wild meadow or lawn. Its cultivars come in white, pink or red. They include the Pomponette Series, which have large double heads; the Rogli Series, which are semi-doubles; and the Tasso Series, which have some of the biggest heads. 'Rose Carpet' has double flowers and 'Habanera' is a double with long petals.

Annuals that can be used as cut flowers

Agrostemma githago	*Gaillardia pulchella*
Alcea rosea	*Gypsophila elegans*
Amaranthus caudatus	*Helianthus annuus*
Antirrhinum majus	*Helipterum roseum*
Brachyscome iberidifolia	*Hesperis*
Calendula officinalis	*Lathyrus odoratus*
Callistephus chinensis	*Limonium sinuatum*
Campanula medium	*Matthiola*
Celosia plumosa	*Moluccella laevis*
Centaurea cyanus	*Nigella damascena*
Chrysanthemum	*Reseda odorata*
Clarkia elegans	*Rudbeckia hirta*
Consolida ambigua	*Salpiglossis*
Coreopsis	*Scabiosa atropurpurea*
Cosmos	*Tagetes erecta*
Dahlia	*Tagetes patula*
Dianthus barbatus	*Tithonia rotundifolia*
Digitalis purpurea	*Xeranthemum annuum*
Erysimum cheiri	*Zinnia elegans*

Bellis perennis 'Pomponette'

Beta vulgaris subsp. *cicla* (leaves)

Bidens ferulifolia 'Golden Goddess'

Beta vulgaris subsp. *cicla* 'Charlotte'

BETA
Beet
This is a small genus of plants that is best known for its vegetables, particularly beetroot. Some of the plants are decorative, including another vegetable, Swiss chard or ruby chard (*B. vulgaris* subsp. *cicla*), which is often grown as a garden plant. With Swiss Chard, it is not the flower that is important but the foliage and the stems. There is also the advantage that they can be eaten.
How to obtain These plants can only be obtained as seed, but nearly all merchants carry them and a number of different varieties are available.
Cultivation Beets will grow in poor soil but the more humus-rich the soil, the better. Z5.

Propagation Sow seed where plants are to grow in early spring, or sow in late summer for winter effects.
Uses These plants are excellent in bedding schemes especially exotic-looking ones. Another perfect use for them is in potagers or decorative vegetable gardens. They look best when they are sited against the sun.

Beta vulgaris subsp. cicla
This is a biennial but it is only kept for the first year since it grows taller and goes to seed in the second. This can be quite dramatic but is difficult to mix in with other plants. There are a number of cultivars. The leaves vary from green to dark purple or red. The stems include shades of yellow, orange, red and purple, as well as green. H 45 cm (18in).

Beta vulgaris subsp. cicla 'Bright Lights'
The stems form a rainbow of different colours, while the foliage is dark green or bronze.

Beta vulgaris subsp. cicla 'Bright Yellow'
This plant produces golden-yellow stems and green leaves which have golden-yellow veins.

Beta vulgaris subsp. cicla 'Bull's Blood'
The foliage of this cultivar is an attractive dark red.

Beta vulgaris subsp. cicla 'Charlotte'
The red stems and red-tinged leaves of this plant have an attractively wrinkled texture.

Beta vulgaris subsp. cicla 'MacGregor's Favourite'
This wonderful plant is prized for its blood-red foliage.

BIDENS
Tickseed
This is a large genus of plants that is closely related to *Cosmos*. The main annual that interests gardeners is *B. ferulifolia* and in it you can see this affinity to cosmos. The golden-yellow flowers are daisy-like with five broad outer petals and a bronze central disc. The leaves are deeply divided and fernlike, making them very decorative. Bidens stems are thin and wiry and have a sprawling habit which makes it perfect for containers. H 30cm (12in) S 60cm (24in).
How to obtain Bidens can be purchased either as seed or as bedding plants from garden centres and nurseries.
Cultivation Any reasonable garden soil will do for bedding plants. For containers a general potting or container compost (soil mix) will suffice. A sunny position is preferred. Z8.
Propagation This plant is really a perennial and it can be kept from one year to the next by taking cuttings and overwintering the young plants. However, it is more convenient to grow new plants from seed sown in early spring under glass.
Uses Bidens can be used in the open garden, either as bedding or in mixed borders. However, their sprawling habit means that they are best employed in containers, especially hanging baskets.

Bidens ferulifolia
This species is mainly grown in its own right. The only commonly available cultivar is 'Golden Goddess' which is not greatly different from the species except that the flowers are a bit bigger.

Other plants There are one or two other species that can be found occasionally. The naming in catalogues varies but the plants are usually sound. *B. humilis* (strictly speaking, *B. triplinervia* var. *macrantha*) is sometimes seen in the form 'Golden Eye'. This is a sprawling, almost prostrate plant that is excellent for hanging baskets. It is similar in appearance to *B. ferulifolia*. *B. aurea* 'Bit-of-Sunshine' also similar.

BORAGO
Borago
A small genus of plants of which only one annual, *B. officinalis*, is commonly grown. One of the perennials, *B. pygmaea*, would make an interesting plant for hanging baskets. *B. officinalis* is often grown as a herb, with the flowers being used as decoration in Pimm's cocktails. It is also now being widely used in the drugs industry

Beta vulgaris subsp. *cicla* (stems)

Bidens ferulifolia

and you can come across fields coloured blue with it. It is of great interest in the garden since it has a long season, with a succession of opening flowers. H 60cm (24in) S 45cm (18in).

How to obtain It is normal to buy borage as seed, which is readily available and easy to grow. You occasionally see plants in pots for sale, but they usually give poor results since borage does not do well in small containers.

Cultivation This plant will grow in most garden conditions. It prefers a sunny spot but will tolerate partial shade. Z7.

Propagation Seed can be sown in pots but it is easier to sow it outdoors in early spring where the plants are to grow. Thin them out to 45cm (18in) intervals. Borage self-sows so once you have it you usually have new plants each year.

Uses Borage makes an attractive addition to herb gardens but it is also very good in mixed borders where it can be used to fill gaps left by spring plants that have faded. It looks pretty in a wild-flower garden.

Borago officinalis

This is a sprawling plant with rough leaves and stems. It produces bright blue flowers that have white centres. They are produced continuously through the summer and into autumn. There is a form *alba* which has white flowers that look very good against the greyish-green stems and leaves. It is perfect for a white colour scheme.

Brachyscome iberidifolia

Borago pygmaea

This is a short-lived perennial which is normally grown as a border plant. However, it has a sprawling nature which might make it worth trying as a biennial in hanging baskets. It has small sky-blue flowers.

BRACHYSCOME
Swan river daisy

This is a large genus of some 70 annual and perennial species which produce daisy-like flowers. Only one of them, *B. iberidifolia*, is widely grown although a few others are occasionally seen. In recent times *B. iberidifolia* is has become one of the most popular annuals, partly because of its looks and partly because of its versatility: it can be used very

effectively in containers as well as making a good bedding plant. The flowers are mainly purple or blue, but some of the cultivars come in different colours including pink and white. H and S 45cm (18in) in good conditions, but most plants are smaller, especially when grown in containers.

How to obtain The best choice of plants comes from growing them from seed since all seed merchants carry at least one version of this. Brachyscomes are also widely available as plants but the choice of flower colour will be restricted, usually to blue. Check plants in flower if you want specific colours since plants are often labelled only as "Brachyscome", sometimes spelt "Brachycome".

Cultivation Plant out after frosts have passed. Any reasonable garden soil will do so long as it is free-draining. Z8.

Propagation Sow seed under glass at 16–18°C (60–64°F) in early spring under glass. In warmer areas the plant self-sows.

Uses Brachyscome is excellent in containers. It can also be used as a bedding plant.

Brachyscome iberidifolia

The main plants have blue or blue-purple outer petals and a yellow central disc. The daisy-like flowers are small, about 2cm (¾in) wide, but are produced in profusion over a long period. The foliage is deeply cut and fernlike.

There are a number of cultivars. In 'Blue Star' the outer petals are rolled back giving the flower a star-like quality. 'Brachy Blue' is a more compact and upright plant. There are several strains with blue, violet, white and pink flowers including Bravo Series and Splendour Series.

Borago officinalis

Annuals for infilling parterres

Ageratum	*Matthiola incana*
Antirrhinum	*Myosotis*
Begonia semperflorens	*Pelargonium*
Bellis	*Plectranthus*
Erysimum	*Primula*
Felicia	*Salvia splendens*
Helichrysum petiolare	*Salvia patens*
Heliotropium	*Tagetes*
Impatiens	*Verbena × hybrida*
Lobelia erinus	*Viola × wittrockiana*

An impressive display of ornamental cabbages (*Brassica oleracea*).

shades of green. The leaves are often fringed.

How to obtain Ornamental cabbages are widely available as seed. They can also be bought as plants in pots. However, if these plants have been in their pots for too long they will make very unsatisfactory plants when planted out.

Cultivation Any reasonable garden soil will suffice. A sunny position is best. Z7.

Propagation Sow seed in spring where the plants are to grow, or sow in a row and transplant when large enough. Brassica seed can also be sown under glass in spring and planted out as soon as possible. Do not keep them in small containers for long.

Uses These plants can be used for winter-bedding schemes when there are few other colourful plants to call on. They are also good in winter containers. Ornamental cabbages can be mixed with edible cabbages in potagers for extra colour. They look particularly effective when partially covered with snow.

Common plants Seed often comes in mixed packets, labelled 'ornamental cabbages' or 'decorative kale', (sometimes 'flowering cabbage, although the plants are on the compost heap before they flower'). Common mixes include 'Northern Lights Mixed', Osaka Series, or 'Kale Sparrow Mix' but many seed merchants offer individual colours by mail order.

Other plants In potagers many of the edible brassicas can look very effective. Red cabbages or curly kale for example. Even cauliflowers (including purple ones) and romanescos are suitable.

BRIZA
Quaking grass

Briza is a genus of around a dozen annual and grasses. Perhaps the best known is *B. media* which is grown as a perennial. However, there are also a couple of annuals which are widely grown. They are called quaking grasses because they have masses of hanging flower heads that look like lockets and which tremble at the slightest hint of a breeze. These are a straw colour; unfortunately, they do not come in the wide range of bright colours that you see in the florists since those have been dyed.

How to obtain Quaking grasses are most commonly available as seed but you will occasionally find plants on sale.

Cultivation Any reasonable garden soil will do so long as it is well-drained. A sunny position is required. Z5.

Propagation Sow the seed where the plants are to grow either in the autumn or in the early spring.

Uses These are mainly used in borders where they mix well with other plants. They can be used to make a delicate edging to a path or border, or in containers. The heads are very good for cutting and drying.

BRASSICA
Ornamental cabbage

This genus is made up of about 30 species, the majority of which are of more interest to the vegetable gardener since they include cabbages, broccolis, Brussels sprouts and cauliflowers, among others. These all belong to the species *B. oleracea*. One might think that there is not much potential here for the flower garden, but in fact there are a number of decorative cabbages and kales that are well worth growing for some winter interest. The leaves come in a wide range of colours including white, cream, pink and purple as well as various

Brassica oleracea (purple-leaved)

Brassica oleracea (green-leaved)

Briza minor

Briza maxima

Sold as the species only since there are no cultivars available. This is the taller of the two annuals. The loose, dangling flower heads are pale green at first, changing to a light straw colour. They are tinged purple. H 60cm (24in) S 25cm (10in).

Briza minor

This is similar to the previous except that the flower spikelets are smaller. H 45cm (18in) S 25cm (10in).

CALCEOLARIA
Slipper flower

A large genus of some 300 species of which there are only a couple of species and a number of cultivars that are of interest to the annual gardener. Their beauty lies in their curious flowers. The lower part is an inflated pouch (giving the plant another of its names – pouch flower) which gives the flower the appearance of a slipper. In the annual varieties the flowers are carried in dense heads, in shades of yellow, gold, orange or red and frequently spotted with red. The bold colours make them ideal for bedding schemes or for bright container arrangements.

How to obtain Slipper flowers can be purchased as either plants in individual pots or as seed. As usual, seed offers a bigger range.
Cultivation Grow in a humus-rich soil that is moisture-retentive but not waterlogged. It should be acid

Calceolaria 'Kentish Hero'

rather than alkaline. Although slipper flowers will grow in sun if the soil is moist enough, they are happiest in light shade. Plant out after frosts have passed. Z9.
Propagation Sow the seed in early spring at 16–18°C (60–64°F) under glass and prick out into individual pots.
Uses These plants are good in containers or bedding, especially in shady sites where bright colours are required. Most make excellent greenhouse plants.

Calceolaria Herbeohybrida Group

This is the main group of hybrids. The flowers come in yellow, orange or red and often have spotted lips. H 20–45cm (8–18in). S up to 30cm (12in).

There are a number of strains with mixed colours including the Anytime Series, 'Bright Bikinis', the Confetti hybrids and the Pocket hybrids. There are also single-coloured varieties including 'Goldcrest' and 'Gold Fever', both with yellow flowers. These plants can be used as greenhouse annuals; in warmer areas they make good bedding and container plants.

Calceolaria integrifolia

These are shrubby perennials, but gardeners normally grow them as annual plants. As perennials they can grow to heights of up to 1.2m (4ft) but as annuals they are more likely to be in the 25–30cm (10–12in) range and about the same across. They produce yellow flowers. The Fructiohybrida Group can be purchased as a mixture or as individual varieties including

Calendula officinalis

'Goldcut', 'Golden Bunch', 'Kentish Hero', 'Midas', 'Sunset' and 'Sunshine'.

CALENDULA
Pot marigolds

There are about 20 species of pot marigolds, but only the annual *C. officinalis* is widely grown. It is commonly called a "pot" marigold because it was once widely used as a herb. Few gardeners use it as such now, although it is still often grown decoratively in herb gardens. At its simplest the flower is a daisy with orange outer petals and an orange or dark central disc. However, there are a number of forms which have semi-double and double flowers. There are also yellow versions. The flowers are up to 10cm (4in) across.

The pot marigold is a useful plant for the garden and it has a certain sturdy quality; it is not a delicate, airy plant. H 75cm (30in) S 45cm (18in). However, its stems can be rather floppy so the real height is often much less.

How to obtain Pot marigolds are best grown from seed, which is readily available. Occasionally plants for sale can be found in garden centres. The plants will self-sow. However they generally revert to the type rather than the particular cultivar planted.
Cultivation Any reasonable garden soil will be sufficient, and although pot marigolds will grow in shade, a sunny position is to be preferred. Z6.
Propagation Seed can be sown where the plants are to be grown, either in autumn or in early spring. Thin plants to intervals of 30–45cm (12–18in).
Uses Pot marigolds are best used as plants for mixed borders, although some of the more compact forms can be used in bedding schemes as well as in containers. They work particularly well in hot-coloured schemes. The flowers are good for cutting.

Calendula officinalis

The species has orange daisies but there are plenty of varieties, such as 'Lemon Queen' which produce yellow ones. The species is grown in its own right but the cultivar 'Radio' is more typical of the garden plant. It has semi-double flowers in which all the petals are orange with no central disc. There are several series including the Kablouna Series, which is tall with double flowers, and the Pacific Beauty Series. Both are mixtures of yellow, gold or orange. Single-coloured cultivars include 'Golden Princess', with golden petals and a black central disc.

Annuals for drying

Amaranthus caudatus	*Helichrysum bracteatum*
Atriplex hortensis	*Hordeum jubatum*
Briza	*Limonium sinuatum*
Centaurea cyanus	*Lunaria annua*
Centaurea moschata	*Moluccella laevis*
Clarkia	*Nicandra physalodes*
Consolida	*Nigella damascena*
Eryngium giganteum	*Onopordum acanthium*
Gomphrena globosa	*Salvia hormium*
Gypsophila elegans	*Xeranthemum annuum*

Callistephus chinensis Milady Series

Campanula medium

CALLISTEPHUS
Chinese aster

This is a single genus species with *C. chinensis* providing a wide range of flowers. It was once much more widely grown than it is now and used to be frequently seen as a cut flower. It is similar to the other asters but the flowers are much bigger, up to 12cm (4½in) or more across. They are either singles or doubles, and come in a wide range of whites, pinks, blues and purples. The singles have a yellow central disc, and they all have a distinctive fragrance. These are bushy, upright plants. H and S 45cm (18in).

How to obtain Chinese asters are more readily obtained as seed but you can still buy plants at some garden centres and nurseries.

Cultivation Chinese asters like a moisture-retentive soil and a sunny position. Z8.

Propagation They can either be sown under glass in early spring at 16–18°C (60–64°F) or in the open ground where the plants are to grow in mid-spring, but these will be later flowering.

Uses They make good bedding plants and can also be grown in mixed borders. Plant in rows in the vegetable garden or an out-of-the-way spot for cutting.

Callistephus chinensis

There is only the one species, but it does have a number of readily available cultivars. The flowers come in the wide range of colours described above, and also in a series of forms. They include the Comet Series, which are compact doubles in a variety of colours, the Giant Singles, 'Craw Krallenaster', which produces flowers with masses of thin petals and the Ostrich Plume Series, which have feathery petals. Others include the dwarf Pinocchio Series, the fine Milady Series, whose flowers have incurving petals, 'Starlight Mix' and the tall Pommax series.

CAMPANULA
Bellflowers

A large genus of more than 300 species of which most are perennials but a number are biennials and annuals. As their name suggests they have bell-shaped flowers, although in the annuals these are often shallow and in some cases look more like saucers than bells. Bellflowers in the wild are mainly blue and occasionally white; in cultivation the annuals tend to have a wider range of colour including pink. The flowers also come as semi-doubles and doubles. They tend to be tallish plants best used in mixed borders rather than low bedding schemes.

How to obtain The best range of plants can be had by buying seed, but there are also plants available from many garden centres and nurseries. Rarer annual seed can be obtained from specialist societies.

Cultivation Any reasonable garden soil will be sufficient so long as it is free-draining. This plant needs sun or light shade. Z6–8.

Propagation Sow seed in early spring under glass. Some can be sown in the open soil where the plants are to grow.

Uses Best used in a mixed border, but some bellflowers can be used in taller bedding schemes.

Campanula incurva

This is a biennial which has low spreading stems and inflated pale blue flowers. H 30cm (12in) S 45cm (18in).

Campanula medium

Canterbury bells are very popular biennial bellflowers. They are available in white, blue or pink and come as singles or the cup-and-saucer doubles. H 60cm (24in) S 30cm (12in). Cultivars include the shorter 'Bells of Holland' and 'Chelsea Pink', with deep pink flowers.

Campanula pyramidalis

A biennial that if grown well produces stems up to 1.5m (5ft) tall, which are covered in blue or white flowers. It is good for growing in pots. S 30cm (12in).

Other plants There are a number of rarer annuals that are worth growing. *C. lusitanica* and *C. patula* form a tangle of thin wiry stems, covered with purple flowers with white centres over a long period. *C. ramosissima* is similar but has thicker stems. *C. thyrsoides* is an upright plant with, unusually, yellow flowers. All these and

Callistephus chinensis 'Ostrich Plume'

Callistephus chinensis 'Starlight Rose'

Campanula pyramidalis

Canna 'Oiseau de Feu'

Canna 'Wyoming'

Canna 'Roi Humbert'

several more attractive plants can be grown in mixed borders or in the rock garden.

CANNA
Indian shot plant

With the growing interest in exotic gardens, cannas have become very popular plants. This is a genus of about 50 species of perennial plants but because they are tender they are treated as annuals. They are dug up every autumn and stored, much in the same way as dahlias are. They are tall plants with attractive large flowers and luscious foliage. The former are carried in spikes and come in bright oranges, reds and yellows, and the latter is usually glossy and sometimes purple or variegated. H 2–3m (6–10ft) S 50cm (20in).
How to obtain Cannas are normally bought as plants or as rhizomes. Seed is available but is generally restricted to mixtures.
Cultivation Plant in a moisture-retentive rich soil in a sunny position. Do not allow them to dry out completely, and lift and store in dry peat substitute after the first frost. Z8.
Propagation Seed can be sown in early spring under glass at 21°C (70°F) after soaking in water. In spring the stored rhizomes can be cut into sections, each with a growing eye, and planted in pots in a warm greenhouse.
Uses Use cannas in exotic bedding schemes or mixed borders where a splash of colour is required.

Canna 'Black Knight'
This eye-catching plant produces a bold display of dark red flowers. H 2m (6ft).

Canna 'Endeavour'
Scarlet flowers are carried on stately plants that reach up to 2.2m (7ft) in height.

Canna indica
This canna has orange or bright red flowers. The leaves are dark green and are often tinged with bronze. There is also an attractive cultivar 'Purpurea', which has purple foliage. H 2m (6ft).

Canna iridiflora
Deep pink flowers are carried on plants that can reach up to 3m (10ft), but are usually less.

Canna 'Striata'

Canna 'Lucifer'
A shorter plant. Spikes of red blooms, touched with yellow. H 60cm (24in).

Canna 'Oiseau de Feu'
This plant has scarlet flowers and dark green leaves. H 1m (3ft).

Canna 'Picasso'
This cultivar has yellow flowers, spotted with red.

Canna 'Roi Humbert'
A dazzling display of orange-red flowers is set against purple foliage. H up to 1.5m (5ft).

Canna 'Striata'
The flowers of this canna are orange and the leaves – pale green with pronounced yellow stripes – set off the orange beautifully. H 1.5m (5ft).

Canna 'Wyoming'
Excellent plants that have purple foliage with darker veins and orange flowers. H up to 2m (6ft).

CELOSIA
Cockscomb

This genus consists of 50 species but the varieties of one species, *C. argentea*, are of most interest. The flowers are so startling that they seem almost artificial in their colouring. There are two types. The commonest (plumosa group) produces upright feathery flowering spikes that look a bit like flames. They come in a variety of reds, oranges, yellows and pinks. The other type (cristata group) produce flat, slightly domed heads with the flowers arranged in curious squiggles, again in bright colours. They can be difficult to place with other plants, but are superb in bedding schemes. H 60cm (24in) S 45cm (18in).
How to obtain Celosias are not so popular as they once were but you can still find plants in some garden centres. There is a good range of seed available.
Cultivation Plant out after the danger of frosts has passed in rich, moisture-retentive soil. A sunny position is required. Z9.
Propagation Sow the seed under glass at 16–18°C (60–64°F) in early spring.
Uses Their main use is as bedding plants in an exotic scheme, but they are also excellent for extra colourful containers.

Celosia argentea 'Apricot Brandy'
This plumosa cultivar has bright orange upright flower heads.

Celosia argentea Century Series
One of the most popular plumosa cultivars, with flowers in a mixture of bright colours.

Celosia argentea 'Fairy Fountains'
The flowers of this plumosa cultivar are less bright and consist of pastel coloured spires.

Celosia argentea 'Freshlock Red'
A plumosa celosia which produces bright red plumes.

Celosia argentea Kurume Series
These are cristata celosia in mixture of bright colours, including some bicolours.

C. argentea plumosa 'Freshlock Red'

Centaurea cyanus

CENTAUREA
Cornflowers

The cornflowers, or knapweeds as they are also known, form a large genus of some 450 species. Many are perennials that are widely grown in our gardens (see page 186). There are also a number of annuals, of which the best known is the common cornflower, *C. cyanus*. These were originally weeds of cornfields, hence the name, and other disturbed ground. They can be grown in borders but still look best when used in a wild-flower garden. They have flattish, circular heads of blue or other coloured flowers Other annual centaureas are quite similar in appearance but are not so commonly seen. H 75cm (30in) S 20cm (8in).
How to obtain The commonest way to buy these is as seed. The rarer plants, need a lot more searching for but they are available from specialist catalogues and societies.
Cultivation Sow in any reasonable garden soil so long as it is free-draining. Full sun is needed. Z6.
Propagation Sow seed where the plants are to flower, in autumn for early flowering or in spring. Thin to 20cm (8in) intervals.
Uses Grow in drifts in mixed borders or as bedding plants. The blue varieties are excellent for wild-flower gardens. Dwarf forms can be used in containers.

Centaurea cyanus
This is the common cornflower. Its flowers are blue, often piercing blue. There is also a wide choice of cultivars which offer a range of flower colours from soft pinks and whites to a very dark purple **that is al**most black. The **cultivated for**ms usually have a lot

more petals, making them almost double. There are also shorter forms, such as the dwarf 'Blue Baby'. 'Black Ball' is very dark purple. In 'Frosty Mixed' the petals have a white edge. Florence Series is a shorter form, and white 'Polka Dot Mixed' is another dwarf form.

Other plants C. americana is similar to the cornflower except that the petals are much more finely cut, giving the flower a very delicate appearance. The flowers are generally white and there are several cultivars. It is not so easy to find but worth the search.

CERINTHE
Cerinthe

This genus of about ten species has been in cultivation for a long time, but it has just been rediscovered and made popular by the seed companies. *C. major* is the particular species that has brought about this popularity. It is a biennial that is grown as much for its foliage as for its flowers. The blue and purple blooms are contained in a spiral, similar to that of the forget-me-not except that the flowers are partially obscured by their sheaths. The plants are quite striking and make excellent displays grown by themselves or mixed with other plants. H 60cm (24in) S 30cm (12in).
How to obtain The best way to obtain these plants is to buy seed from merchants. You can buy

Cerinthe major

plants but they are not very satisfactory as they tend to grow spindly. Once you have planted cerinthes, they will often self-sow.
Cultivation Any reasonable garden soil so long as it is free-draining. A sunny position is required. Z5.
Propagation Sow seed in autumn or spring where the plants are to flower or in pots under cool glass. Prick them out but do not leave them in small pots too long.
Uses Cerinthes can be used in a mixed border or as bedding. They are excellent for gravel gardens and can be used in containers.

Cerinthe major
This is the main species grown. It has green leaves that are often white spotted, especially when young. The form 'Purpurascens' has much bluer leaves and is the form mostly grown. The partially obscured flowers are purple.

Cerinthe major 'Kiwi Blue'

There are some new varieties appearing, such as 'Kiwi Blue', but they are not much different.

Other plants Cerinthe minor is much rarer but it makes an excellent foliage plant since its leaves are white spotted. The flowers are small and yellow. It appears as *C. minor aurea* 'Bouquet Gold' in some catalogues.

CHRYSANTHEMUM
Chrysanthemum

There can be few gardeners who do not know chrysanthemums. As well as the well-known cultivars there are 20 species, including annuals and perennials. We do grow some annuals in our gardens but the main form – florists' chrysanthemum – is a perennial. However, because of its tender nature we treat it as an annual and replant it each year. Florists' chrysanthemums are now highly developed: there are ten basic types, each having many cultivars. They are grown as border or

Cerinthe major set off against a wall beautifully.

Chrysanthemum 'Southway Swan'

Chrysanthemum 'Curtain Call'

Chrysanthemum 'Glamour'

Chrysanthemum 'Primrose Allouise'

Chrysanthemum segetum 'Prado'

decorative plants, but the majority are cultivated either for cutting or for exhibition. Many gardeners become hooked on them and often turn over a large part of their garden to growing them. The annual chrysanthemums are grown more for their effect in the garden. With such diversity, this is a genus well worth getting to know.

How to obtain Florists' chrysanthemums are sold as small plants in garden centres and nurseries. There are several mail-order nurseries that specialize in them. There was a short period a few years ago when they were classified as *Dendranthema*. Although they are now called *Chrysanthemum* again, some catalogues may still list them under their former name. Other chrysanthemums are usually sold as seed and they can be found in most seed merchants' catalogues.

Cultivation Plant out chrysanthemums once the threat of frost has passed. They need a soil that has been enriched with plenty of well-rotted organic material.

The soil should be moist but free-draining. A sunny position is needed. Z: see individual types.

Propagation Propagate florists' chrysanthemums from cuttings taken from the newly emerging basal growth on plants that have been overwintered. Other types are grown from seed sown in early spring at 13–16°C (55–60°F) under glass. It can also be sown where the plants are to grow, but this will make flowering later.

Uses Florists' chrysanthemums, can be grown in mixed borders, but they are more often grown in rows for cutting or for exhibition purposes. They are also good plants for containers. Other chrysanthemums can be used in mixed borders or as bedding. Corn marigolds (*C. segetum*) are excellent plants for the wild-flower garden.

Florists' chrysanthemums

There are thousands of these to choose from and it is best to get catalogues from the specialist

nurseries to see the range available. The ten basic types have flowers that vary from singles to doubles. There are also "incurved" chrysanthemums, which have a ball of upward curving petals, and "reflexed" ones, which have petals that curve downwards. There is a wide range of colours including white, yellows, oranges, red, pinks and purples. H 1.5m (5ft) S 75cm (30in). Z4.

Chrysanthemum carinatum

These plants have single, daisy-like flowers. The outer petals come in a range of colours from white to yellow, and orange to red. There is often an inner ring of colour at the base of the petals and a central disc of brown. 'Court Jesters' is a good mixture. There are some double forms. H 60cm (24in) S 30cm (12in). Z7.

Chrysanthemum coronarium

These are bushy plants which produce single daisy-like flowers. They have yellow outer petals and yellow central discs. The green foliage is very finely cut and fern-like in appearance. These chrysanthemums look good in wild-flower meadows. H 75cm (30in) S 45cm (18in). Z7.

Chrysanthemum segetum

Corn marigolds have simple daisy-like flowers with golden outer petals and a golden central disc. They are very beautiful when seen *en masse*. Some cultivars, such as 'Prado', have extra-large flowers and a dark disc. 'Eastern Star' has paler yellow petals and a dark central disc. Excellent for wild-flower gardens. H 60cm (24in) S 30cm (12in). Z8.

Chrysanthemum tenuiloba

A plant with extremely finely cut foliage and yellow outer petals and discs. This is a sprawling plant that produces a mass of foliage speckled with yellow. It has a cultivar 'Golden Fleck'. H 30cm (12in).

Chrysanthemum 'Debonair'

Chrysanthemum 'Taffy'

Chrysanthemum 'George Griffiths'

Chrysanthemum carinatum

Chrysanthemum tenuiloba

Cladanthus arabicus 'Criss-Cross'

CLADANTHUS
Palm Springs daisy

This is a small genus of daisy-like flowers of which only one, *C. arabicus,* is grown. It is not often seen and yet it is excellent for hanging baskets and other containers. Fortunately it is being offered by an increasing number of seed merchants and it is worth seeking out seed.

The light green leaves have very thin leaflets and create a tangled nest for the flowers. Both the leaves and the flowers are fragrant. The flowers are daisies with yellow outer petals and a yellow central disc. They nestle right down in the foliage, a characteristic that distinguishes this plant from the annual chrysanthemums it resembles in other respects. Another distinctive feature is that from just beneath each flower emerges a few more stems, each in turn carrying more flowers so the plant gets bigger and bigger. H up to 45cm (18in) or more, S 40cm (16in).

How to obtain This plant is mainly grown from seed, which is distributed by an increasing number of seed merchants. Occasionally you will see plants for sale in some garden centres.

Cultivation Any reasonable garden soil will be sufficient, so long as it is free-draining. Centaureas need a sunny position. Z7.

Propagation Seed should be sown in early spring under glass at 13–16°C (55–60°F). It can be sown later where the plants are to grow, but flowering will be later.

Uses They work well in window boxes, hanging baskets or other containers, or they can be used in bedding schemes.

Cladanthus arabicus

This is the only species in general cultivation. It is sold both as the species, described above, and as the cultivars 'Criss-Cross' and 'Golden Crown'. These are similar to the species but produce slightly larger flowers.

CLARKIA
Clarkia

This is a medium-sized genus of 36 species of which several are grown in our gardens as annuals. They include a number of plants that were previously classified as *Godetia* and under which name many gardeners still know them.

They are a mixed bunch with some having large single or double flowers, while others are quite small but are carried in sufficient quantities to make the plants attractive. Their basic form is funnel-shaped. The predominant colour is pink although some are dark enough to be called red or purple. Many are tinged with lighter or darker colour. Clarkias produce lots of flowers over a long period, so they are good for bedding or for use in containers. H 45cm (18in) S 30cm (12in).

How to obtain Clarkias are widely available as seed although many catalogues still list some species as *Godetia*. Most garden centres also sell plants in individual pots.

Cultivation Clarkias will grow in any reasonable garden soil, but it must not be too rich and it must be free-draining. These plants grow best in a sunny position but they will also tolerate a little light shade. Z7.

Propagation Seed can be sown in early spring where the plants are to grow. For earlier flowering, the seed can either be sown in the open in autumn or under glass in early spring at a temperature of 13–16°C (55–60°F).

Uses They make excellent bedding plants especially when they are planted in blocks or drifts. They can also be used in containers such as pots or tubs.

Clarkia 'Blood Red'

Clarkia amoena

This is the satin flower, which is often listed as *Godetia amoena*. The upward-facing flowers are quite large, up to 5cm (2in) across. They are single or double, and come in various shades of soft pink. There are a number of cultivars including the Grace Series and Satin Series (dwarf), both of which have mixed shades. 'Rembrandt' is tall with rose and white flowers, 'Sybil Sherwood' has salmon-pink flowers, and 'Memoria' has pure white ones. 'Furora' has bright red blooms, and 'Blood Red' has blood-red flowers with pale centres.

Clarkia bottae

This pretty plant is not as brash as the previous species. It has simple cup-like flowers in pink with a pale centre. It is often listed as *Godetia bottae*. There are also several cultivars.

Clarkia breweri (C. concinna)

The flowers are wide, with thin, deeply cut petals in shades of pink. The best known cultivar is 'Pink Ribbons'.

CLEOME
Spider flower

A surprising large genus with 150 species. Only one of them, *C. hassleriana*, is grown to any extent in our gardens, although with a bit of searching the enthusiast will discover several others in this intriguing genus. The flowers are carried in rounded spikes at the top of tall stems. The heads are quite unlike those of any other plant: the

Cleome hassleriana 'Helen Campbell'

Cleome hassleriana 'Pink Queen'

spikes are quite loose and open and below them are the seed pots of flowers that have already faded. They are carried on very thin stems, giving the plant its characteristic "spider" look. The flowers are scented and they come in pink, white or mauve. The heads are usually slightly darker in colour towards the top where the buds have yet to open. The foliage is a bit like that of the lupin. H 1.5m (5ft) S 45cm (18in).
How to obtain Cleomes can be bought as plants. However, they do not like to remain in pots too long so it is best to obtain them as seed, of which there is usually a greater range available.
Cultivation Plant out after the danger of frosts has passed. Cleomes need a fairly rich soil that is very free-draining in full sun. They can also be grown under glass for cutting. Z10.
Propagation Sow in early spring under glass at a temperature of 18°C (64°F).

Uses These plants look best when grown in drifts either in a mixed border or as bedding. They can be used as cut flowers.

Cleome hassleriana
This is the species that is most commonly seen. It is occasionally grown as a species, but more commonly as one of the several available cultivars. Seed catalogues often list it under all manner of names which are no longer extant. 'Colour Fountain' is a mixture of colours but there are also varieties which are restricted to one colour such as 'Cherry Queen' (carmine red), 'Helen Campbell' (white) 'Orchid Queen' (pale mauve) and 'Pink Queen' (pink).

Other plants If you search you will find a number of other cleomes being offered by one or two seed merchants and specialist societies, *C. aculeata, C. gynandra* and *C. serrulata* amongst them. These have smaller flower heads so they are not as showy as *C. hassleriana*, but the structure and colour range is roughly the same.

COBAEA
Cathedral bells
This genus contains about 20 species of perennial climbers, of which one, *C. scandens*, is of interest to gardeners. Although a perennial it is generally treated as an annual. Its great attraction, apart from its purple bell-shaped flowers, is that it is one of the few annual climbers. It can reach up to 4.5m (15ft) in the year if started off early enough, although as a perennial it can eventually grow as tall as 20m (70ft).

Cobaea scandens growing up a willow tripod.

How to obtain Most seed merchants carry seed. Sometimes you find plants at garden centres and nurseries. These should be planted out quickly since they do not do well in small pots.
Cultivation Plant in a humus-rich soil that is neutral to alkaline. A warm sunny site is needed. Do not plant out until after the danger of frosts has passed. Z9.
Propagation Raise plants from seed, sown in early spring under glass at 25°C (77°F).
Uses Cobaea does best when planted against a warm wall, either growing up a support or through another plant. It can be also used over pergolas and trellising.

Cobaea scandens
The flowers are large, attractive bells that stick out horizontally from the stems. They open whitish-green and quickly change to a deep purple. The form *alba*

has white flowers. *Cobaea scandens* is often known as the cup and saucer plant, the cup being the flower and the saucer the green calyx around its base.

Cobaea scandens

Annuals for light shade

Begonia semperflorens	Mimulus
Cleome spinosa	Myosotis
Consolida ambigua	Nemophila menziesii
Cynoglossum amabile	Nicotiana
Digitalis purpurea	Oenothera biennis
Erysimum cheiri	Pelargonium
Lobelia erinus	Schizanthus
Lobularia maritima	Senecio cineraria
Lunaria annua	Thunbergia alata
Matthiola bicornis	Viola × wittrockiana

Collinsia bicolor 'Blushing Rose'

COLLINSIA
Collinsia

This is a genus of about 20 plants of which only one is in general cultivation. This is *C. bicolor*, or *C. heterophylla* as it is sometimes called. It is not related to the lupin, but at a quick glance it could be mistaken for one, albeit a small one. It produces spikes of flowers of which the lower lip is one colour (usually purple) and the upper another (usually white or pink). The pointed leaves are more like those of a penstemon and rise stalkless direct from the stems. Although these plants are generally upright, they can be slightly floppy. It is best to plant them closely together so that they give each other support, or you can give individual plants other support, such as short, twiggy branches. H 60cm (24in) S 30cm (12in).

How to obtain Collinsias are rarely seen as plants in garden centres and it is best to buy them as seed from one of the few merchants that stock it.

Cultivation The soil should be a humus-rich one, but it should be free-draining. Collinsias prefer full sun, but they will grow in a little light shade. Z7.

Propagation Sow seed where the plants are to grow in spring, or in autumn for earlier flowering. Thin to 30cm (12in) intervals.

Uses Collinsias can be used either in drifts as bedding or in a mixed border. They are shown to good effect in a wild-flower garden.

Collinsia bicolor

This is the main plant grown and is described above. 'Candidissima' is a form with all-white flowers. There are also mixtures on offer from some seed merchants. They include 'Blushing Rose' and 'Surprise', which produces an attractive combination of blue, lilac and rose-pink flowers.

Other plants The only other species that is sometimes offered is *C. grandiflora*. It is a shorter plant than the above and much bushier. It also has bicoloured flowers, with a blue-purple lower lip and a paler upper one.

There are a few seed merchants that offer this species; otherwise you need to look to specialist societies in order to find it.

Collomia grandiflora

COLLOMIA
Collomia

A genus of about 15 species of which a couple are occasionally cultivated. The most frequently grown is *C. grandiflora*, although it is still rarely seen. Very few seed merchants carry the seed and it is mainly grown by gardeners to whom the seed has been handed down from generation to generation. It is an old-fashioned cottage-garden plant of great beauty and it is a pity it is not more readily available. Once established you rarely lose it since it is self-sowing, often forming large drifts. However, it is easy to remove if it is in the wrong place. H 1m (3ft) S 60cm (24in), when growing well.

How to obtain Collomia seed is not easy to come by, although some seed merchants do stock it now. It is also available from some specialist societies.

Cultivation This plant does best in a rich, moist soil, which should be free-draining. A sunny position is required. Z7.

Propagation Sow seed in early spring where the plants are to grow. After the first year it self-sows if allowed to seed. Thin plants to 30cm (12in) intervals.

Uses Collomia could be used as a bedding plant, but the flowering season is short and it is best grown as drifts in a mixed border.

Collomia grandiflora

This is an upright, branched annual with red stems that contrast well with the mid green leaves. The flowers are a creamy salmon-pink and are carried in clusters or whorls at the tips of the branches. The seed heads are somewhat sticky and it is best to let them dry before trying to extract the seed.

Other plants Collomia *biflora* is a similar, but shorter annual with smaller heads of red or orange flowers. It is more colourful than the above but has less presence.

CONSOLIDA
Larkspur

A genus of about 40 species of annuals which used to be included in the genus *Delphinium*. The naming is still in a state of flux and the main larkspur grown may be called *C. ambigua* or *C. ajacis* depending on which authority you consult. This confusion is carried on in the seed catalogues, so don't give up if you can't find the plants under the first heading you try. Whatever their names, the plants are excellent annuals. They

Consolida ajacis, mixed colours

Consolida ajacis 'Frosted Skies'

Convolvulus tricolor 'Royal Ensign'

look like miniature delphiniums but the flower spikes are much more open and delicate; the flowers seem to float like butterflies. There is quite a range of colour. Blue is the predominant one but there are also pinks and whites and some bicolors. The plants vary considerably in size from dwarf varieties that are only 30cm (12in) high to tall ones 1.2m (4ft) high. S 30cm (12in).
How to obtain Larkspurs are available both as plants in individual pots and seed from which a bigger range is available.
Cultivation Grow in any reasonable garden soil as long as it is free-draining. A sunny position is required. Taller forms may need some form of staking in exposed positions. Z7.

Consolida ajacis

Propagation Sow seeds in the position where the plants are to grow in early spring. Thin to 30cm (12in) intervals.
Uses Good for bedding and mixed borders, these plants can also be grown in pots and tubs. The taller varieties make very attractive cut flowers.

Consolida ajacis
This is the main species and it has large number of cultivars. Some are light and airy while others have much more compact, denser flower spikes, often with double blooms. There are several series which provide a mixtures of colours. For example there are the Dwarf Hyacinth Series, Dwarf Rocket Series and the Giant Imperial Series, all providing double flowers in a range of colours and heights. 'Frosted Skies' is a beautiful single with white and blue flowers. 'Sublime' is another tall variety, as is 'Earl Grey'; both come in mixture of colours. 'Kingsize Scarlet' produces very good red flowers.

CONVOLVULUS
Bindweed
An enormous genus of some 250 plants, of which many are weeds that you would not want near your garden. However there are one or two excellent garden plants. *C. tricolor* is one of these. As well as having attractive flowers it has the added bonus of being one of the few annuals that climb.

How to obtain Convolvulus are grown from seed which is very widely available.
Cultivation Grow convolvulus in any reasonable garden soil, so long as it is free-draining. A sunny site is needed. Z8.
Propagation Sow under glass in the early spring at 13–18°C (55–64°F). They can also be sown *in situ*, although the plants will then flower later, and so will not grow quite as vigorously.
Uses These plants are excellent for growing up any form of trellising or up wigwams of sticks, either in borders or in pots or tubs.

Convolvulus tricolor
This attractive plant has the typical funnel-shaped flowers of the convolvulus. Here they are a rich dark blue, with white markings at the base of the petals and a yellow eye. H 40cm (16in) S 30cm (12in). The plant is most often seen in the form 'Royal Ensign' which has very deep blue flowers. Seed can also be bought in mixtures which contain white and pink flowers as well as blue.

Other plants Convolvulus sabatius must be one of the most beautiful of all container plants. It is a tender perennial that is treated as an annual and either overwintered under glass or started again each year. It produces a profusion of small, funnel-shaped sky-blue flowers that smother the small, shrubby plant. It is usually bought as a plant rather than seed. A real gem.

Convolvulus sabatius

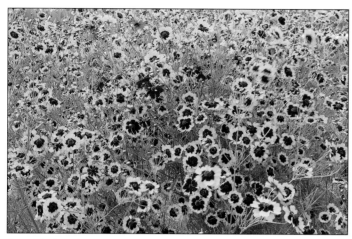

Coreopsis tinctoria

Cosmos bipinnatus 'Sonata Pink'

COREOPSIS
Tickseed

A large genus of up to 100 species of both annuals and perennials. The perennials are dealt with elsewhere. *C. grandiflora* and *C. tinctoria* are the plants of interest to the annual gardener. The flowers are daisies with golden-yellowish outer petals and a gold central disc. The ends of the petals are usually fringed. Some plants have simple single flowers; others have semi or fully double blooms. The flowers are quite large, up to 6cm (2½in) in diameter. The plants vary in height from low-growing ones that reach only 23cm (9in) to ones that are 1.2m (4ft) tall; most reach about 45cm (18in) in height and spread.

How to obtain Annual coreopsis can occasionally be bought as plants from garden centres but they are best purchased as seed.

Cultivation Grow in any reasonable garden soil. Coreopsis prefers a sunny position, but the plants will take a little shade. Z7.

Propagation The seed can be sown in the early spring under glass at 13–16°C (55–60°F), or sown directly into the soil where the plants are to grow.

Uses They can be used in drifts in mixed borders or in bedding schemes. The shorter varieties can also be used in containers such as pots and tubs. Taller varieties are good for cutting.

Coreopsis grandiflora

This is a perennial that is usually treated as an annual. Seed of the species is commonly available but the plant is more frequently grown as one of the many cultivars including 'Early Sunrise' (semi-double flowers), 'Gold Star' (quilled petals) and 'Sunray' (double flowers).

Coreopsis tinctoria

This is similar to the previous species, but it has slightly smaller flowers. There is also more variety in the colour with the central disc often being reddish-brown and the petals flushed with red and brown. Again, it has plenty of cultivars. They include 'Tiger Flower', a dwarf only 23cm (9in) tall, and 'Mahogany Midget' a slightly taller plant which has rich mahogany-coloured flowers. Various mixed-coloured plants are also sold by some seed companies.

COSMOS
Cosmos

This is one of those annuals that has maintained its popularity over the years. There are 25 species but there are only a couple of annuals which are grown regularly. However, both have a number of cultivars, so there is plenty to interest the annual gardener. They have daisy-like flowers but the petals are wide, so producing an almost continuous disc. The petal colours are mainly white and pink in *C. bipinnatus*, the main species, but there are some yellow variants in the other species, *C. sulphureus*, as its name might suggest. Plants vary in height from the dwarf at about 30cm (12in) to the tall at up to 1.5m (5ft).

How to obtain Cosmos can be obtained as plants from most garden centres. However, they need to be purchased early on since they soon become leggy (producing long, bare stems) in small pots. It is better to raise them as seed.

Cultivation Cosmos will grow in any reasonable garden soil, but they like full sun. Z8.

Propagation Sow in early spring under glass at 16–18°C (60–64°F) or slightly later where the plants are to grow.

Coreopsis grandiflora 'Early Sunrise'

Cosmos growing in a mixed border.

Cosmos sulphureus

Uses They can be grown either as bedding plants or in drifts in a mixed border. Single colours look better in the latter. They make good cut flowers.

Cosmos bipinnatus

This is the most commonly grown species. It has a range of single colours as well as one or two varieties with bicolours: 'Candy Stripe', with its white flowers with crimson edging, is one example. The Sensation Series is one of the most popular with large flower heads up to 9cm (3½in) across. Sonata Series is a dwarf form, which grows only 30cm (12in) high. They can both be bought as a mixture or as individual colours such as 'Sonata Pink'. 'Sea Shells' has curious quilled petals. 'White Swan' is a beautiful white variety.

CREPIS
Hawk's Beard

This is a large genus of about 200 species or annuals and perennials. Most are considered weeds but some perennials are grown in the garden along with a couple of annuals, only one of which is in general cultivation. This one, *C. rubra*, is a gem and ought to be grown more widely than it is.

All the crepis have flower heads similar to those of the dandelion. However, unlike the dandelion, crepis are generally well-behaved and do not seed everywhere. (If the dandelion did not sow itself so prodigiously it would also be welcome since it is a magnificent

plant.) Crepis make good bedding when they are grown *en masse*, but these plants are also suitable for filling gaps in mixed borders, especially along the margins.

How to obtain These plants are usually only available as seed from seed merchants. Very occasionally you see plants for sale but do not rely on finding them.

Cultivation Plant out in any reasonable garden soil so long as it is free-draining. Z6.

Propagation You should sow the seed in pots as soon as it is ripe. No heat is required for raising these seeds.

Uses Crepis are excellent in mixed borders and in gravel gardens. They are also attractive when used as bedding plants or in a variety of tubs or pots.

Crepis rubra

This has single dandelion-like flower heads of sugary pink, which float on wiry stems above a rosette of hairy leaves for a long period during summer. H up to 40cm (16in), but often much less, S 20cm (8in). There are a few cultivars of which the white form 'Alba' is the best. There is also a darker pink form, 'Rosea'.

Other plants There are one or two more species that are occasionally grown, but it is usually not as easy to get hold of their seed. The flowers of these species are less showy. Most are yellow-flowered and look good if grown in a meadow garden. Examples include *C. biennis* and *C. capillaris*.

Crepis rubra

Cuphea ignea 'Variegata'

CUPHEA
Cuphea

Not all gardeners know this genus but it is a big one containing about 260 species. Quite a number of these are grown in gardens, usually as annuals even if they are perennials or shrubs. The best known is probably *C. ignea*, known as the cigar flower. The colours vary but red is common and gives the plants a bright cheerfulness that makes them ideal for bedding or for growing in containers. If they are plants you do not know it might be worth experimenting with one or two of them, especially if you like exotic borders.

How to obtain Cuphea is widely available from seed merchants, but check catalogues carefully since naming may vary. You sometimes see plants in garden centres.

Cultivation Cupheas will grow in any reasonably fertile garden soil,

but it needs to be free-draining. They prefer a sunny position but they will also grow in a lightly shaded one. Z9.

Propagation Sow seed in the early spring under glass at 13–16°C (55–60°F). The seed can also be sown where the plants are to grow, but flowering will be later.

Uses They make excellent bedding, especially in colourful, exotic schemes. They can also be used in containers and in mixed borders.

Cuphea cyanaea

This perennial is quite commonly grown as an annual. It has masses of orange tubular flowers with yellow tips. H 1m (3ft).

Cuphea ignea

This is the most common cuphea. It has bright red tubular flowers with a deep red and white mouth that looks rather like the ash on the tip of the cigar. It will grow up to 75cm (30in) as a perennial but is often less when grown as an annual. The variety 'Variegata' has leaves splashed with cream.

Other plants *C. hyssopifolia* (false heather) is a rounded shrub often treated as an annual. The tubes are much more flared, producing open flowers in either white or pink. H and S 60cm (24in) high.

Cuphea × purpurea is another shrub grown as an annual. These flowers are also widely flared, making them appear larger than those of the more common varieties. The colour varies from pink to red; there are also purple varieties. H up to 75cm (30in).

Cynoglossum amabile 'Mystery Rose'

Dahlia 'Bishop of Llandaff'

Dahlia 'Lilliput'

Dahlia 'Hamari Katrina'

CYNOGLOSSUM
Hound's tongue

A genus of about 55 species, most of which are annuals or short-lived perennials. The flowers are generally quite small but there is plenty of them and they are a lovely blue – a colour not often seen in bedding plants. They are related to the forget-me-not; as with that plant, a progression of flowers open from a spiral of buds.

How to obtain Cynoglossums are most frequently seen as seed.

Cultivation These plants are best grown in any reasonable garden soil that is moisture-retentive but at the same time free-draining. They prefer sun but tolerate a little shade. Z7.

Propagation Sow seed in pots in spring. No heat is required. They can also be sown in the open ground where they are to flower.

Uses Cynoglossums work well as bedding plants or when placed in a mixed border.

Cynoglossum amabile

This is the most commonly grown annual in the genus. As well as the blue flowers of the species, there are also varieties with white or pink flowers, some named, such as 'Mystery Rose' (rose-pink) or 'Avalanche' (white). H 60cm (24in), but often much less, S 30cm (12in).

Other plants Cynoglossum officinale is a biennial with deep purple flowers. It is best grown in the wild-flower garden.

DAHLIA
Dahlia

Most gardeners will not need to be told what dahlias are: they are very familiar to us all. While there are only 20 species there are a colossal 20,000 cultivars, which shows just how popular they are. They are not only grown in decorative situations in the garden but also for cutting and for exhibition purposes. The flowers are usually quite large and blowsy in a variety of bright colours.

The shape of the flower head has been divided into eleven groups varying from simple singles to double, spherical ones known as pompoms. There are other doubles, such as the cactus dahlia in which the narrow petals curve upwards. These plants are all perennials that are treated as annuals; they are lifted each autumn and stored overwinter before replanting in spring. There are also a few varieties which are grown from seed each year. Bedding dahlias only grow to about 45cm (18in) or so but the

Dahlia 'Brilliant Eye'

perennial ones will grow up to 1.5m (5ft) in height and 60cm (24in) in spread.

How to obtain Dahlias are sold as tubers from most garden centres. They are also available from specialist nurseries which offer a much larger choice and are a must for anyone who becomes interested in these plants. Their catalogues are often a mine of information. The bedding varieties are available from most seed merchants, and most carry a good range.

Cultivation Grow dahlias in a moist humus-rich soil that is free draining. Choose a sunny position. Stake taller varieties. Z9.

Propagation The tubers can be cut in half once growth has just begun, leaving a shoot on each piece. Alternatively take basal cuttings from the emerging shoots. Seed can be sown under glass in early spring at 13–16°C (55–60°F).

Uses Many gardeners grow dahlias in separate beds or in rows in the vegetable garden for cutting or

Dahlia 'Cactus Video'

for exhibitions. They can also be grown in mixed borders. The smaller annuals make good bedding plants and can also be grown in containers.

More common plants

There are so many varieties of dahlia that it is difficult even to start listing them. There are some, such as purple-foliaged 'Bishop of Llandaff', which are used more frequently in borders than they are for exhibition, while others, such as 'Hamari Gold', are mainly grown for exhibition purposes, but can also be used as a cut flower or even as a decorative variety in the border.

Other plants The annual bedding varieties grown from seed are offered by most seed merchants. They are usually offered as a mixture of colours. The well-known dwarf 'Redskin' has dark red or bronze foliage and flowers in a variety of colours. 'Coltness Mixed' is another old favourite.

DATURA
Thorn apple

This is a small genus from which the shrubby species have been reclassified as *Brugmansia*. The

Dahlia 'Decorative'

Dianthus barbatus 'Harbinger Mixed'

Dianthus barbatus 'Scarlet Beauty'

Dianthus chinensis 'Pluto Karminrosa'

Dianthus chinensis 'Merry-go-Round'

annual and perennial ones remain, however, as *Datura*. These plants are beautiful but they contain toxic substances; if eaten they are likely to be fatal. So plant them only if you feel confident that no one will suffer any ill effects. Their beauty lies in the very large trumpet flowers, which are white or soft pastel colours. Some have a wonderful scent. The plants are large, open plants. H 1m (3ft) S 60cm (24in).

How to obtain Most garden centres are reluctant to sell these plants because of their toxic nature. The best way to obtain them is from seed merchants.

Cultivation Plant out after the threat of frost has passed. The soil should be fertile but free-draining. The site should be sunny. Z: see individual entries.

Propagation Sow the seed under glass in early spring at 16–18°C (60–64°F). Grow the plants on in containers.

Uses Datura are mainly grown as container plants, and they are suitable for large pots or tubs.

They can be planted in the open soil. The poisonous nature of the plant means that it needs to be sited carefully.

Datura inoxia

This is another relatively common species. It has trumpets that are white, or white tinged with violet. They are very fragrant. It is slightly less hardy. Z9.

Datura stramonium

Known as Jimson weed, this is the main species grown. It has large white trumpets which are mainly white, but are occasionally purple. The seed capsules are large, green and prickly, hence its other name of common thorn apple. Z7.

DIANTHUS
Dianthus

This is a well-known genus with more than 300 species and an unknown number of cultivars. It is best known for the perennials which include carnations and pinks. However, there are a number of annuals, which are

mainly used as bedding plants. Although these are not quite as popular as they once were, they are still widely grown. The flowers are either single, semi-double or double in a range of bright colours, of which only blue is missing. They are often scented. Most are annuals, the notable exception being the biennial *D. barbatus*, the sweet William, which has to be sown one year for flowering the next.

How to obtain Most annual dianthus can be purchased as either seed or plants. Seed generally offers a better range of possibilities.

Cultivation Any reasonably fertile garden soil will do but it must be free-draining. A sunny position is required. Z: see individual entries.

Propagation Sow seed of annuals in early spring under glass at 13–16°C (55–60°F), or outside where the plants are to grow, but these will be later flowering. Biennials should be sown outside in drill in early summer and moved to their flowering positions in autumn.

Uses Annual dianthus are mainly used either as bedding or in a mixed border. Some can be used as container plants.

Dianthus barbatus

This is the biennial sweet William. It is the upright plant and the tallest of the annuals. It is deliciously scented. It has flat heads of red, pink or white flowers, which are often patterned. It is good for cutting. H 70cm (28in) S 30cm (12in).

Dianthus chinensis

One of the most commonly seen annual pinks. It is variously known as the Chinese, Japanese or Indian pink. It carries single flowers that are red, pink or white with a darker central eye and often patterns. The petals are fringed. H and S 30cm (12in).

This plant has given rise to a number of cultivars with 'Strawberry Parfait' being one of the most popular. Heddweigii Group is also widely grown. Z7.

Other plants Other species that are frequently grown as annuals, often as cultivars, include *D. armeria*, the Deptford pink, and *D. superbus* which has very deeply cut petals.

Dianthus barbatus

Dianthus chinensis 'Strawberry Parfait'

Dianthus 'Can Can Scarlet'

Digitalis purpurea

Digitalis purpurea (mixed colours)

DIGITALIS
Foxgloves

This well-known genus consists of more than 20 species, most of which are perennials but some are annuals or treated as such. The common foxglove, *D. purpurea* is one of these. It usually grows in the wild as a perennial in mainland Europe but, oddly enough, only grows as a biennial in Britain.

Foxgloves are tall, erect plants with spikes of tubular flowers that create a wonderful effect in the border. They look especially good when grown as a drift, but also look fine dotted throughout an informal planting.

How to obtain Foxgloves can occasionally be found as plants in garden centres or nurseries but they are best grown from seed which is readily available from a number of sources.

Cultivation These plants will grow in any garden soil, in either full sun or a partially shaded position. Cut off the flower spikes before they seed if you wish to prevent self-sowing. Z4.

Propagation The seed can be scattered where the plants are to grow as soon as it is ripe. Once you have foxgloves in your garden, they will continue to self-sow if they are allowed to seed.

Uses Foxgloves work best in mixed borders although the cultivars can look good used in bedding schemes. The wild forms are excellent in wild-flower gardens. Foxgloves also make very good cut flowers.

Digitalis purpurea

This is the common foxglove and it is a superb garden plant that is well worth growing. The flowers are a soft pinkish-purple with darker spots inside. There is also a white form *albiflora*. H 2m (6ft) S 45cm (18 in).

The cultivars are much brasher, with bigger flowers that are more densely packed on the stem. There is a wider range of pinks and whites and the spots are usually larger. The Excelsior hybrids (or Suttons Excelsior hybrids) provide the main range of cultivars. The Foxy hybrids are about half the size of the species.

Other plants *Digitalis lanata* is a perennial that is often treated as an annual. It produces small flowers, which are white with soft brown veining.

Digitalis purpurea f. albiflora

DIMORPHOTHECA
African daisy

This was once a much larger genus because *Osteospermum* was included in it and plants of that genus are still sometimes listed as *Dimorphotheca*. The plants have rather beautiful daisy-like flowers which come in a range of white and oranges, usually with a purple central disc and a central ring of violet-purple at the base of the petals. They come from South Africa and they need sunshine to open. They usually shut in the evening so they are not good plants for people who see their gardens only in the evening. They are sprawling plants so do not reach any great height. H 30cm (12in) S 45cm (18in).

How to obtain These are commonly available as plants from garden centres and nurseries. The plants often do not have any cultivar name attached to them; if you want specific colours, buy them in flower. They can also be purchased as seed from various seed merchants.

Cultivation These plants will grow in any reasonable garden soil so long as it is free-draining. They must have a warm, sunny position or the flowers will not open. Z9.

Propagation Sow African daisy seed under glass at 18°C (64°F) in the early spring.

Uses These are mainly used as bedding plants but they can also be used for filling spaces towards the front of a mixed border. They can also be used in tubs.

Dimorphotheca sinuata

This is probably the most commonly grown plant in the genus. The species itself is not often seen; it is more commonly grown as one of the hybrids. The flowers are white, orange, yellow or even pink, often with a touch of blue or purple at the base of the petals.

Dimorphotheca sinuata

Annuals for edging lawns and paths

Ageratum
Bellis
Begonia semperflorens
Brachyscome
Clarkia
Crepis rubra
Dianthus chinensis
Felicia
Iberis amara
Limnanthes douglasii
Lobelia
Lobularia maritima
Myosotis
Nemesia
Nicotiana
Petunia
Primula
Silene pendula
Tagetes
Viola × *wittrockiana*

Other plants *Dimorphotheca pluvalis* is known as the rain prophet because it shuts up in cloudy conditions. The flowers are white with a blue base to their petals.

DIPSACUS
Teasel

There are about 15 species in this genus which consists mainly of biennials. They are not the most colourful plants but there are a couple that are welcome in our gardens. The attraction is mainly due to the structure of the plant. It is a tall, upright, open-branched plant which has a stately architectural quality about it. The stems and leaves are covered in stout prickles and the large,

Dipsacus fullonum (foliage)

Dipsacus fullonum

opposite leaves join at the stem forming a large cup which is usually filled with water. H 2m (6ft) S 1m (3ft).

How to obtain Teasels have tap roots which means that they do not do well in pots. As a result, they are rarely seen for sale as plants. However, they are generally available as seed.

Cultivation Teasels will grow in any reasonable garden soil. They do best in sun but will also grow in light shade. Z3.

Propagation Sow the seed in the open ground where the plants are to grow in autumn or spring.

Uses These plants work well at the back of a mixed border in an informal garden, but they look best in a wild-flower garden. The seed heads make good winter decoration in the garden as well as providing winter feed for several species of bird. They make excellent dried flowers.

Dipsacus fullonum

This is the wild teasel which is the plant most commonly seen. The flower heads are egg-shaped and rather prickly with spine-like bracts. The flowers first open as a band round the middle and then expand both upwards and downwards. They are a pale purple colour, which contrasts well with the pale green of the flower head. They flower in their second year.

Other plants *Dipsacus sativus* This is the fuller's teasel, the head of which was used to tease out wool

Dorotheanthus bellidiformis 'Gelato Pink'

and raise the nap on cloth. The spines on the head are hooked at the end, just perfect for the job.

DOROTHEANTHUS
Livingstone daisy

A genus of about ten species which are still more commonly known under the name *Mesembryanthemum*. Only one of these is generally cultivated. It was once more widely grown than it is now, but it is very suitable for coastal gardens and is still frequently seen as bedding plants around the coast. The plants are low growing with narrow succulent fleshy leaves and masses of brightly coloured daisies. The flowers are up to 4cm (1½in) diameter. Unfortunately the flowers tend to shut up in dull weather. H 15cm (6in) S 30cm (12in) or more.

How to obtain Livingstone daisies are frequently sold as plants either in bedding packs or in individual pots. They are also readily available as seed from most merchants, and are often listed under the name *Mesembryanthemum*.

Cultivation These plants thrive in well-drained sandy soil, including pure sand, but they will happily grow in most well-drained garden soils. A sunny position must be provided or the flowers will not open. Z9.

Propagation Sow the seed under glass at 16–18°C (60–64°F) in the early spring.

Uses Excellent for bedding and borders in coastal regions where the light is bright and the soil

usually well drained. They can also be used very successfully as bedding or in containers.

Dorotheanthus bellidiformis

This is the species usually grown. The daisy flowers have a brown central disc and narrow petals in a wide range of colours including yellow, pinks, reds, purples and whites. They are often two-toned with, say, pink petals flushed with white from the centre.

There are a number of cultivars: some, like 'Magic Carpet' are a mixture of colours, while others such as 'Gelato Pink' (pink), 'Apricot Shimmer' (soft apricot), 'Cape Sunshine' (bright yellow) or 'Lunette' (also called 'Yellow Ice', pale yellow) are single-coloured varieties.

Other plants There are several other species of which seed is available if you search for it. The most frequently seen is *D. gramineus*. Its flowers are similar to *D. bellidiformis* but the leaves are narrow and grass-like.

Dorotheanthus bellidiformis

Eccremocarpus scaber

ECCREMOCARPUS
Chilean glory flower

This is a small genus containing five species of perennial climbing plants of which one, *E. scaber*, is regularly seen in gardens. It is debatable whether this should be classified in gardening terms as a perennial or as an annual since it is regularly treated as both. However, the majority of gardeners use it as an annual climber, unless it is grown in a glasshouse or conservatory, and so it has been included here. It is fast growing and so well suited for use as an annual. It will grow up through other plants or up twiggy supports up to 5m (15ft) if used as a perennial. As an annual it reaches 2–3m (6–10ft).
How to obtain Chilean glory flowers are occasionally seen in pots but they are more frequently sold as seed. Most seed merchants carry them.
Cultivation These plants will grow well in a reasonably fertile, well-drained soil. A sunny position is needed. If they are planted against a warm wall, the plants may overwinter and produce flowers for a second year. Z9.
Propagation Sow seed in early spring under glass at 13–16°C (55–60°F).
Uses Grow as a climbing plant either in borders or against walls or fences. Chilean glory flowers can also be grown in large containers if supported by a wigwam of sticks or a framework.

Eccremocarpus scaber

This is the main species grown. It is usually grown as the straight species, which has orange or flame-red tubular flower carried in loose heads. However, there are

Echium vulgare

also a number of named cultivars available. These include the Anglia hybrids which offer a range of mixed colours such as pink, red, orange and yellow. Tresco hybrids also include crimson and cream flowers. Some seed merchants just label seeds under their colours – for example, "yellow forms" – without giving a cultivar name.

ECHIUM
Bugloss

A large genus containing about 40 species, which provides the gardener with several excellent plants. They vary considerably in size from low bedding plants of about 45cm (18in) to giants reaching up to 2m (6ft) or even more. However, close examination will show that although the size and shape of the plants are different, the flowers are all basically funnel-shaped. They are

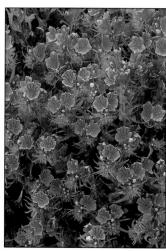

Echium vulgare 'Blue Bedder'

usually blue although they also come in other colours. This is a beautiful group of plants, especially the larger ones.
How to obtain The bedding varieties are sometimes available as plants. The others have to be bought as seed. You may have to search to find it but it is becoming more widely available.
Cultivation Plant in a fertile soil that is well drained. The larger varieties appreciate a richer soil, but, again, it must be well-drained. The smaller ones need full sun but some of the bigger ones will also do well in a dappled shade. Z: see individual entries.
Propagation Sow the seed under glass at 13–16°C (55–60°F) in early spring. The smaller ones can be sown where they are to flower.
Uses The smaller plants make excellent bedding. The taller ones are architectural in shape. They

stand out as features in borders or look good in informal planting under trees or among shrubs.

Echium vulgare

This is the most frequently seen species. The species itself is called the common viper's bugloss and is excellent for wild-flower gardens. It has a tall spike or spikes of flowers which appear from ever-expanding coils. They are blue but purple in bud. H 1m (3ft) S 30cm (12in). There are various bedding forms derived from this, including 'Blue Bedder' which has light blue flowers that darken with age. Dwarf hybrids include pink and purple flowers. Z5.

Other plants Echium wildpretii is typical of the larger species. It forms a rosette from which emerges a tall spike up to 2m (6ft) in height; it is densely covered with blue flowers and has a rather exotic appearance. S 45cm (18in). Similar species are *E. simplex*, *E. fastuosum*, *E. candicans* and *E. pininana*. These are plants for the specialist grower but well worth the effort. Z9.

EMILIA
Tassel flower

There are about 24 species of annuals in this genus, of which a couple are widely grown in our gardens. The brightly coloured flowers are carried singly or in clusters, held above the leaves. They are upward-facing and look rather like miniature tassels or paint brushes (in the past this

Emilia coccinea 'Scarlet Magic'

A particularly fine display of *Emilia coccinea*.

plant was also called Flora's paint brush). H 60cm (24in) S nearly the same as the height.

How to obtain Tassel flowers are mainly found as seed, either at garden centres or from seed merchants' catalogues. The seed is sometimes still listed under its old name of *Cacalia*.

Cultivation Any reasonable garden soil will suffice so long as the ground is free-draining. A sunny position is required. Z9.

Propagation Sow the seed in early spring at 13–16°C (55–60°F) under glass, or later directly into the soil where the plants are to grow. The latter method provides plants that are later flowering.

Uses These make good bedding plants but they also work very well in drifts of a single colour in a mixed border. They are excellent for cutting and can be dried.

Emilia coccinea

This is the most frequently seen plant. The flowers are a bright flame-red. Sometimes they are sold as cultivars such as 'Scarlet Magic' but these are not greatly different from the species.

Emilia sonchifolia

This is a bit more varied than the above. The main flower colour is reddish-purple, but there are also orange, scarlet and yellow forms available. They are usually sold as mixed colours.

Other plants There are a number of other species that are available if you search for them. They include

EE. atriplicifolia, glabra, hastata and *suavolens*. However, they do not vary greatly from the above.

ERYNGIUM
Sea holly

This is a very large genus of some 230 species of which the vast majority are perennials. However, there are a few biennials, of which one is wildly grown in gardens. This is *E. giganteum*. It is a prickly beast but a plant of such beauty that it is worth putting up with this negative aspect. Its leaves, stems and bracts are a silvery green. It is often known as Miss Willmott's ghost: this venerable gardener had the habit of surreptitiously dropping seed in her friends' gardens and so a trail of plants were left in her footsteps – her "ghost". The name is doubly apt because the plant shows up ghostly white at night.

Eryngium giganteum 'Silver Ghost'

How to obtain This is a tap-rooted plant that does not do very well in pots. It is best to avoid buying potted plants unless they are very young, and to go for seed which is readily available.

Cultivation Any well-drained garden soil is suitable, even poor ones. Full sun is preferred. Z6.

Propagation Sow the seed in spring where the plant is to grow. It will flower the following year. Sea holly self-sows if left to set seed.

Uses This plant is best used in a mixed border where it can be grown in a drift or in single plants. It does well in a wild-flower garden and is particularly good in gravel gardens. Excellent as a dried flower.

Eryngium giganteum

This is the plant described above. The flowers are contained in dome-shaped heads which are greenish-blue in colour. Some merchants list 'Miss Willmott's Ghost' as a cultivar name but this is the common name for the form generally in cultivation and is no different from plants or seed sold simply under the name of the species. H 1m (3ft) S 36cm (14in). The cultivar 'Silver Ghost' has been introduced relatively recently. This is an attractive plant that is much more silvery-white than the species.

Other plants Of the other biennials, *E. campestre* is the one you are most likely to find. This is a plant of dunes and dry grassy places. It is not so spectacular as other eryngiums but it is still a good plant for wild gardens and gravel gardens. It is smaller than the above, 60cm (24in) high and almost as wide. The flower heads are greenish and relatively small.

Eryngium giganteum is an excellent plant for drying.

Erysimum helveticum

ERYSIMUM
Wallflower

This is a large and popular genus of about 200 species. Most of the plants are perennials but they are not long lived so they are often treated as biennials, especially the common bedding forms. Wallflowers actually do grow well on walls, which is the nearest garden equivalent to their native cliffs; this is because they like a well-drained position. If they are given such conditions in the garden they will last for several years. The bedding varieties are very colourful and cheerful and have a very distinctive scent which is one of the pleasures of spring. H 75cm (30in) S 40cm (16in).
How to obtain The bedding varieties are widely sold as bare-rooted plants: they can be found everywhere from garden centres to petrol stations. However, it is often difficult to know what the flower colour will be. Seed merchants give a much larger choice of cultivars and allow you to be certain of the colour.
Cultivation Any good garden soil will suffice, but a well-drained one will ensure that plants overwinter better. Wallflowers prefer a sunny position. Z7.
Propagation Sow seed in rows in early summer and transfer to their flowering position in autumn.
Uses They make excellent bedding plants, and can also be used in mixed borders or in containers such as pots. They look good in cottage-garden schemes, and also combine well with bulbs.

Erysimum × allionii
This is the Siberian wallflower, which produces bright orange flowers. It is commonly available but it is not seen so often now as the following species. There are no cultivars available.

Erysimum cheiri
This is the main bedding wallflower. It is a wonderful plant, very fragrant and colourful, and the one from which most of the bedding wallflowers have been derived. Seed is mainly sold as named cultivars. Some of these, such as Bedder Series, are sold as mixtures or individual colours such as 'Orange Bedder' or 'Blood Red'.

Other plants There are several other species that can be used as annuals. One delightful little plant is *E. helveticum* which has bright yellow flowers that open from purple buds. It self-sows, so once you have it there is no need to re-sow; simply transplant the seedlings if necessary.

ESCHSCHOLZIA
Californian poppy

This small genus of about ten species produces a couple of annuals which are stalwarts of the border. They have typical poppy flowers which are shallow, funnel- or saucer-shaped, and with petals that look fragile, although they are not quite so crumpled as many of the poppies. These are cheerful flowers which come in plenty of bright colours, with orange as the base colour. The foliage is finely cut. The plants are rather sprawling and the flowers are carried on thin stems well above the leaves. H and S 30cm (12in).
How to obtain Californian poppies can be purchased as plants but they are best bought as seed which is readily available.

Eschscholzia californica 'Mikado'

Cultivation Californian poppies can be grown in any reasonable garden soil so long as it is free-draining. They need a sunny position. Z6.
Propagation Seed can be sown in late spring where the plants are to grow. The plants will self-sow for future years. However, the cultivars are likely to revert to the basic species.
Uses These plants can either be used in bedding schemes or in mixed borders.

Eschscholzia californica
This is the main species grown. The species has mainly orange flowers but there are several cultivars which have blooms of yellow, flame-red, red and pink. There are also doubles and semi-doubles, whose flowers are more

Eschscholzia californica 'Mission Bells'

tissue-like. 'Ballerina' has double and semi-double flowers in a mixture of colours; 'Apricot Flambeau' is a pretty apricot semi-double with splashes of red; 'Mission Bells' is also semi-double but comes in a mixture of colours; 'Cherry Ripe' has red petals that get paler towards the centres; 'Mikado' has deep orange petals, which are scarlet on the reverse side; and 'Alba' is a beautiful creamy-white.

Other plants *Eschscholzia caespitosa* are similar to the above but with slightly smaller, yellow flowers. The best known cultivar is 'Sundew', which has beautiful lemon-yellow flowers.

EUPHORBIA
Spurge

This is a colossal genus with more than 2,000 species ranging from annuals to trees. The majority grown in gardens are perennials or shrubs that are treated as perennials. However, there are also two annual plants, *E. lathyris* (the caper spurge) and *E. marginata* (snow on the mountain), that make a welcome contribution to our gardens. These are both upright plants but they are quite dissimilar in other respects. Like all euphorbias, these plants produce a latex sap which can cause severe irritation to the skin and so they should only be handled wearing gardening gloves. Be sure to keep the juice away from eyes. No parts should be eaten, especially the seed of *E. lathyris* which looks a bit like capers (hence its name) but which is highly toxic.

How to obtain Both the annual species are occasionally offered as plants but they do not do very well in small pots so it is best to grow them from seed. This is readily available.

Cultivation Grow in a reasonably rich soil – the richer the soil the bigger the plants will grow. A sunny position is best. Z4–8.

Propagation Sow where the plants are to grow. *E. lathyris* will self sow if left to set seed.

Uses *E. lathyris* is best grown in a mixed border where its shape can be appreciated. *E. marginata* can also be used there, and it makes a good bedding plant.

Euphorbia lathyris

An upright but a much sturdier plant than the following. It produces side branches, giving it a candelabra shape and great architectural presence when fully grown. Excellent for bringing structure to a border. H 1.5m (5ft) S 45cm (18in).

Euphorbia marginata

An upright plant which has ovate leaves and tiny flowers carried among bracts at the top of the stems. These bracts and top leaves are either variegated in white or totally white, hence its common name of snow on the mountain. H 1m (3ft) S 50cm (20in). There are several cultivars including 'Summer Icicle', 'Icicle' 'Kilimanjaro' and 'Snow Top'.

EUSTOMA
Prairie gentian

A small genus of three species, of which one is increasingly being grown. Its new popularity is partly

Eustoma grandiflorum

due to the fact that it has become more readily available as a cut flower, which has prompted people to start growing it. Until recently the genus was called *Lisianthus* and the plant is still often called this. It is an erect plant bearing upward-facing flowers that are cup-shaped and often semi-doubles or doubles. The common name prairie gentian comes from the flower's blue or purple colour.

How to obtain The best way of obtaining the prairie gentian is as seed which is widely available.

Cultivation These plants are often grown under glass for cutting purposes, but they can also be grown outside once the threat of frost has passed. Grow in a reasonably fertile, free-draining soil. It should preferably be neutral to alkaline. A warm, sunny position is important. Z9.

Propagation Sow the seed under glass at 16–18°C (55–60°F) in the late winter.

Uses The prairie gentian can be used as a decorative plant in a mixed border or it can be grown simply for cutting purposes.

Eustoma grandiflorum

This, the only species grown, is sometimes called *E. russellianum* or *Lisianthus russellianus*. The cup- or bell-shaped flowers are purple or blue in the species and have a wonderful satiny texture. The centres are darker. H 1m (3ft) S 30cm (12in).

There are a number of cultivars which offer a larger range of colours including pink, white, red and even yellow. 'Echo Pink' is a double pink. 'Aloha Deep Red' is, as its name suggests, red. Heidi Series are single cultivars in a wide range of colours including salmon and various picotees. Echo Series are doubles, again with picotees. Double Eagle Mixed is another double with a mix of colours. All are good choices for cutting.

Euphorbia marginata

Fragrant annuals

Brachyscome iberidifolia	Ipomoea alba
Centaurea moschata	Lathyrus odoratus
Datura	Lobularia maritima
Dianthus barbatus	Matthiola
Dianthus chinensis	Nicotiana
Erysimum cheiri	Oenothera
Exacum affine	Pelargonium (foliage)
Heliotropium arborescens	Phacelia
Hesperis matronalis	Reseda odorata
Iberis amara	Viola × wittrockiana

Exacum affine

EXACUM
Persian violet

This is a genus containing about 25 species, only one of which is used as an annual in our gardens. This one, *E. affine*, has been used for a long time as a bedding plant and is still popular. The flowers are shallow dishes or saucers and are generally coloured a soft blue-purple with a yellow centre. Cultivars offer a slightly wider range of colours. As an added bonus the flowers are scented. These are bushy plants, which can grow up to 75cm (30in) high; the bedding or pot-plant cultivars are usually 30cm (12in) tall or less. S 15cm (6in).

How to obtain Persian violets can be purchased as plants, either in individual pots or in bedding packs. They can also be obtained as seed, where a wider range of plants is available.

Cultivation Plant out once the threat of frosts and chilly nights are definitely over. Persian violets will grow in any reasonable garden soil so long as it is free-draining. They need a warm and sunny position. Z9.

Propagation Sow seed at 18–20°C (64–68°F) under glass in the early spring.

Uses In the garden they can be used as bedding, where their uniform height can be exploited.

They can also be used as container plants for both tubs and pots, and for window boxes. In the house or greenhouse they can also be used as pot plants.

Exacum affine

This is the only species grown. The species is sometimes grown in its own right, but it usually appears in the form of one of the cultivars. The majority have soft blue-purple flowers but some are darker blue, pink and white. The bedding varieties are quite short, with many being no more than 15cm (6in) high: the height is reflected in names such as 'Midget' and 'White Midget'.

FAGOPYRUM
Buckwheat

This is genus of about 15 species of which a couple of annuals are grown both in agriculture and gardens. They are very similar to the plants that were once classified as *Polygonum* (the persicarias) and they have at times been listed as such. The flowers are small and carried in clusters and usually pink or white.

These plants have been in cultivation since the earliest agriculture as a source of grain and they are still used for green fodder and making flour. In the garden they are long flowering, lasting from midsummer well into

the autumn. Although they are perhaps not as popular as they once were, seed is still available.

How to obtain It is doubtful whether you will find buckweat as plants, but quite a number of seed merchants carry stocks of seed. However, you may need to search for it.

Cultivation Any reasonable garden soil will suffice. A sunny position is best. Z7.

Propagation Sow the seed in spring in open ground where the plants are to grow. They are usually best sown in drifts rather than as individual plants.

Uses Their long flowering period makes these plants useful in a variety of places in the garden including informal beds and wild-flower borders. They are widely grown in the herb garden and still used to treat a variety of ailments. Bees love the flowers so they are good plants for honey producers. They also make good green manure, for which purpose they are often sold.

Fagopyrum esculentum

This has clusters of white or pink flowers carried on erect, knotted stems that also contain green, heart-shaped leaves. The flowers are fragrant. H 60cm (24in) S 30cm (12in).

Other plants *Fagopyrum tartaricum* is the Indian or Tartary buckwheat, and also known as *Polygonum tartaricum*. It is similar to the above but about half its size. It is more tolerant of drought conditions and makes excellent dried flowers.

FELICIA
Blue daisy

A large genus containing about 80 perennials and shrubs as well as a few annuals. A couple of these are among some of the most popular of bedding plants, while others are also quite widely grown. As their common name suggests they have daisy-like flowers with blue petals. The central discs are a good, contrasting yellow. They produce masses of small flowers over a long period. If grown under glass many will survive longer than a

Fagopyrum esculentum

A massed display of *Felicia amelloides*.

Felicia amelloides

year since they are strictly speaking short-lived perennials rather than annuals. Here they will grow up to 60cm (24in) high or more, but in the open they are normally much shorter. They are bushy plants and they grow about as wide as they are tall.

How to obtain Felicias can be obtained as plants from garden centres or nurseries and they are widely available as seed from all seed merchants.

Cultivation Plant out once the threat of late frosts has passed. Felicia will grow in any reasonable garden soil, although it must be free-draining. It is important to grow these plants in a warm, sunny position. Z9.

Propagation Sow seed in the early spring under glass at 16–18°C (60–80°F).

Uses Felicias have a wide range of uses. They work very well in bedding schemes but can also be used in mixed borders. They also make excellent container plants.

Felicia amelloides

A very good plant with blue flowers of varying shades. It is often sold as one of the many varieties which come in white as well as blue. 'Read's White' is a good example of the former. There is also a form with white variegations on the leaves known as 'Santa Anita Variegated'.

Felicia amoena

This is a slightly smaller plant than the previous species, but again it has bright blue flowers. Its form 'Variegata' is one of the best-known felicias; the leaves are heavily variegated with cream markings, and set off the blue flowers beautifully.

Felicia bergeriana

This is one of the lowest-growing felicias, reaching only about 25cm (10in) in height. Like the others it has blue flowers. This blue gives it its common name, the kingfisher daisy.

Felicia heterophylla

A mat-forming plant with blue daisies. However, this species also produces some pink cultivars, such as 'The Rose'. It also has a white variety 'Snowmass'.

GAILLARDIA
Blanket flower

There are about 30 species in this genus, and they comprise both annuals and perennials. There is one annual that is widely grown, as well as a perennial that is often treated as an annual. Like a large number of annuals, these plants are members of the daisy family and they exhibit the typical daisy-like flowers of an outer ring of petals and an inner disc. The petals are usually yellow in colour, flushed red towards their base and with reddish or brown central discs. These are big powerful daisies, up to 14cm (5½in) across in some plants. They are always eye-catching and more than earn their keep in the garden. H 60cm (24in) S 30cm (12in).

How to obtain Blanket flowers are available both as plants from garden centres and seed from a wide variety of sources.

Cultivation Plant out in any reasonable-quality garden soil. They should be placed in a warm and sunny position. Z: see individual entries.

Propagation Sow seed under glass in early spring at 13–16°C (55–60°F). It can also be sown where the plants are to flower, but the flowering will be much later than in greenhouse-raised plants.

Uses These make excellent bedding plants and they can also be used in a mixed border, especially one devoted to hot colours.

Gaillardia × grandiflora

This is strictly speaking a perennial and is often grown as such in warmer areas. However, it is also widely grown as an annual. It has the largest flowers. There are a number of cultivars including: 'Burgunder' (red flowers), 'Dazzler' (flame-red and yellow) and the similar 'Wirral Flame'. Z4.

Gaillardia pulchella

This is an annual which has smaller flowers than the previous but they are the same colour. There are several cultivars including 'Summer Prairie', 'Red Plume' and 'Yellow Plume'. Z8.

Red-flowered annuals

Adonis aestivalis	*Dianthus chinensis* 'Fire Carpet'
Alcea rosea 'Scarlet'	*Linum grandiflorum*
Amaranthus caudata	*Malope trifida* 'Vulcan'
Antirrhinum 'Scarlet Giant'	*Nicotiana* 'Crimson'
Begonia semperflorens 'Lucifer'	*Papaver rhoeas*
Cleome spinosa 'Cherry Queen'	*Pelargonium*
Cosmos bipinnatus 'Pied Piper Red'	*Salvia splendens*
	Tagetes patula 'Cinnabar'
	Verbena 'Blaze'

Gaillardia pulchella 'Summer Fire'

Galactites tomentosa

Gazania 'Mini-Star Tangerine'

Gazania hybrids

GALACTITES
Galactites

This is a small genus of only three plants, of which just one, *G. tomentosa*, is grown. It is not often seen, which is surprising because it is a wonderful plant. The fact that it is a thistle may put a lot of people off, but it is a well-behaved thistle. Like other thistles it does self-sow, but only gently – in fact, there never seem to be enough seedlings to go round. This is an open, bushy plant with bluish-green leaves that are heavily marked with silver lines. The flowers are typically thistle-shaped and of a soft purple that contrasts beautifully with the variegated foliage. The foliage and stems do have sharp spines. There are no cultivars, but the flowers and variegated foliage are good enough to make them unnecessary. H up to 1m (3ft), but often only half of this. S 45cm (18in) in bigger plants.

How to obtain Galactites are not very easy to find but a few suppliers, including specialist societies, stock the seed. It is well worth seeking out.

Cultivation Any reasonable garden soil will suffice, so long as it is free-draining. The plants should

have a sunny position, but they will tolerate a little light shade, for example a position in which they grow partially under a rose bush. Z6.

Propagation Sow the seed where the plants are to grow in autumn or spring, or sow in pots in an open frame. Galactites will self-sow if left to set seed, but they rarely become a nuisance.

Uses Galactites are excellent plants for the mixed border, especially if you have a garden with a silver colour scheme. They also do very well in gravel gardens.

GAZANIA
Gazania

This is a genus consisting of about 16 species of which none is commonly grown. However, between them they have produced a number of hybrids which are very popular among gardeners, especially in coastal gardens where there is bright light. This light is essential as gazanias have a habit of shutting up in dull weather.

The flowers are daisy-like with colourful ring of outer, pointed petals and a golden central disc. There is a wide range of colours from brilliant yellow through orange to various red and pinks.

There is often an inner ring of darker colour. The flowers are carried singly on stems above green foliage which is slightly frosted with silver. Gazanias make excellent bedding plants. H and S 25cm (10in).

How to obtain These are widely available as plants in garden centres and nurseries as well as seed. Seed offers the largest range of possibilities.

Cultivation Plant out after the threat of frosts has passed in a well-drained soil, preferably a light, sandy one. Gazanias require a warm, sunny position. Z9.

Propagation Sow seed under glass at 18–20°C (64–68°F) in the early spring.

Uses Gazanias are good plants for containers, such as window boxes, where they can be used to great effect. However, their main use is as colourful bedding plants.

Gazania Chansonette Series
A mixture of colours including several different pinks and oranges, bronze and yellow.

Gazania 'Cream Beauty'
As its name suggests, this lovely cultivar produces flowers of a creamy white colour.

Gazania Daybreak Series
This is another series with a wide range of colours. Some colours are sold separately, as in the form 'Daybreak Bronze'.

Gazania Kiss Series
The flower colours in this series include golden-yellow, bronze, rose and white. The colours are available separately.

Gazania 'Magenta Green'
This cultivar produces flowers of deep purple.

Galactites tomentosa (foliage)

Gazania 'Daybreak Bronze'

Gazania hybrids

Gazania hybrids

Gazania **Mini-Star Series**
This series produces flowers in another wide range of colours including white and pink. The plants also come in single colours: for example, 'Mini-Star Tangerine' and 'Mini-Star White'.

Gazania **'Orange Beauty'**
The flowers of this plant are bright orange in colour.

Gazania **'Snuggle Bunny'**
This cultivar produces blooms of an unusual bronzy-orange.

Gazania **'Sunshine Mixed'**
This plant carries daisies in a gay mixture of colours.

Gazania **'Talent Mixed'**
This mixture produces flowers in plenty of different colours, and has attractive grey-silver foliage.

GERANIUM
Geranium

This is a very large genus of some 300 species, many of which are grown as perennials, especially by enthusiasts. There are also a couple of annuals worth growing. They are not the most spectacular of geraniums and will probably not appeal to the average gardener, but they do add another

Pink-flowered annuals

Alcea rosea 'Rose'
Callistephus chinensis
Clarkia
Crepis rubra
Diascia
Dianthus
Godetia grandiflora 'Satin
    Pink'
Helichrysum bracteatum
    'Rose'
Lathyrus odoratus
Lavatera trimestris
Nicotiana 'Domino
    Salmon-Pink'
Nigella damascena 'Miss
    Jekyll Pink'
Papaver somniferum
Silene pendula 'Peach
    Blossom'

Geranium lucidum

couple of plants to the enthusiast's garden. They are especially suitable in a wild area, as they can spread a little too quickly in most gardens. The flowers are shallow saucers or funnels and are generally some shade of purple. Pelargoniums (see page 77) were removed from this genus more than 100 years ago, but they are still often referred to as geraniums.
How to obtain You very rarely see plants offered, although nurseries that specialize in geraniums may occasionally sell them. Seed is also difficult to find, but it is offered by specialist societies.
Cultivation Any garden soil will do. These plants will grow in either sun or shade. Z7.
Propagation Sow the seed in spring where the plants are to flower. Geranium seed can also be sown in pots and placed in an open frame without heat.
Uses These plants are quite rampant, so they are best grown in a wild garden. If used elsewhere, thin as necessary.

Geranium bohemicum
This plant forms a dense, untidy mat. The foliage is hairy and the small flowers are violet-blue. It is biennial and self-sows. H 30cm (12in) or more, S 15cm (6in).

Geranium lucidum
This is grown for its foliage, which is round and, unlike that of most geraniums, glossy and succulent-looking. The plant is excellent in shady areas since it helps to illuminate the darker

areas. In autumn it takes on reddish tints and the stems are also red. The flowers are small and pink. It is a very attractive plant, but it does seed everywhere. It is perfect for the wild or woodland garden. H 25cm (10in) S 15cm (6in).

GILIA
Gilia

A genus of about 30 species, consisting mainly of annuals. Two or three of these are in general cultivation. They vary from those with tight clustered heads of small flowers to those with loose heads of open saucer-shaped flowers. The predominant colour is blue. These look best when grown *en masse*, particularly in meadow garden. They are not seen as frequently as they once were but they are still widely available. H 60cm (24in) S 30cm (12in).

Gilia capitata

How to obtain Seed is readily available from a number of seed merchants. Occasionally you will find plants available for sale.
Cultivation Any reasonable garden soil will suffice, but it should be well-drained and not too rich. Z8.
Propagation Sow the seed in the autumn or spring in the open ground where the plants are to grow. They often self-sow if the conditions are warm enough.
Uses Gilias can be used as massed bedding or planted in drifts in mixed border. Their untidy habit makes them particularly good for wild gardens, especially meadows.

Gilia capitata
This is the main species grown. It has spherical heads (4cm/1½in across) of lavender-blue flowers, over finely cut foliage. They are sometimes known as Queen Anne's thimbles. A white form, 'Alba', is occasionally offered.

Gilia tricolor
This is called birds' eyes because the flowers have a central eye. The simple, saucer-shaped flowers have blue petals and yellow or orange shades in the throat. This, too, has a white variety, 'Alba'.

Other plants Once there were 25 or so gilia commonly available, but this has been reduced to those above. *G. achilleifolia*, which has finely cut foliage, is sometimes seen. It is a sprawling plant with spherical heads of blue flowers similar to those of *G. capitata*.

Gladiolus 'Seraphin'

GLADIOLUS
Gladiolus

A once-popular genus for which enthusiasm has dwindled in recent years. However, many gardeners still grow gladiolus, so it is still widely available. There are about 180 species, some of which are treated as perennials while others are treated as tender annuals. Generally it is the hybrids that are grown. In spite of their decline there are still around 10,000 of these from which to choose – only a few of them are listed here. They consist of tall plants with sword-like leaves and spikes of tightly packed flowers. These are shaped like open trumpets or funnels and come in almost every colour. Some are pure colours while others are bicoloured. H 1.5m (5ft) S 15cm (6in).
How to obtain Corms are readily available from most garden centres and nurseries, usually in packs showing the colour. General bulb firms and specialist nurseries also sell gladioli, with the latter providing the biggest selection as well as offering catalogues which give advice on cultivation.
Cultivation These plants need a well-drained but reasonably fertile soil. They should have a position in full sun. Lift the corms after the leaves die back and store in a dry, frost-free place. Stake plants in exposed positions. Z8.
Propagation The small cormlets can be divided from their parents when the plants are dormant.
Uses Gladioli can be used in a decorative border but they are often grown in a special bed or in rows in the vegetable garden for cutting or for exhibition. They make excellent cut flowers.

Gladiolus 'Charm'
A fine gladiolus suitable for the border. It has simple, pinkish-purple flowers with white throats.

Gladiolus 'Elvira'
This is another simple gladiolus whose flowers come in pink. It is early flowering.

Gladiolus 'Florence C'
A large-flowered variety which produces dense spikes of glistening white, ruffled flowers

Gladiolus 'Green Woodpecker'
The spikes of greenish-yellow flowers have bright red markings in the throat.

Gladiolus 'Kristin'
The flowers of this cultivar are large, ruffled and white.

Gladiolus 'Nymph'
An early-flowering gladiolus that is suitable for the border. It has white flowers edged with red.

Gladiolus 'Prins Claus'
This is another good border variety. It has pure white flowers that have cerise markings.

Gladiolus 'Royal Dutch'
This is a large-flowered variety which carries pale blue flowers with white throats.

Gladiolus 'Seraphin'
This attractive plant has soft pink flowers with white throats.

GLAUCIUM
Horned poppy

This is a genus containing about 25 species of annuals and short-lived perennials, which are usually treated as annuals. The flowers are open and dish-shaped, with petals that look like fragile tissue paper. They come in colours ranging from yellow to orange and red. These plants are called horned poppies because of the shape of their seed pods, which are long and curved. They can be used as bedding, but are generally used in mixed borders. The height varies.
How to obtain Glauciums are occasionally sold as plants but they are tap-rooted and soon become starved in small pots. It is best to grow them from seed, which is quite widely available.
Cultivation Any garden soil will do, but glauciums need good drainage and full sun. Z7.
Propagation Sow the seed in autumn or spring where the plants are to flower.
Uses They are used to great effect in mixed borders and gravel gardens. The latter suits them very well.

Glaucium corniculatum
This is the red horned poppy. It is a biennial and produces red or orange flowers over silvery foliage. H and S 38cm (15in).

Glaucium flavum

Glaucium flavum
This is the yellow horned poppy. It is a perennial plant but is usually treated as an annual, although in well-drained conditions it will survive into a second year. The flowers are yellow or orange in colour. H 60cm (24in) S 45cm (18in).

Glaucium grandiflorum
This is another perennial grown as an annual. It has orange to deep red flowers.

GOMPHRENA
Gomphrena

A large genus containing almost 100 species, of which most are annuals although only one is in general cultivation. This, along with another couple of now-forgotten species, were once more popular than they are now. Their

Gomphrena globosa dark form

Gomphrena globosa pale form

decline is mainly down to the reduced appeal of summer bedding. They have egg-shaped flower heads densely packed with pink, red, purple or white bracts. **How to obtain** Gomphrenas are best purchased as seed from one of the several seed merchants that sell it.

Cultivation Plant out in any reasonable garden soil, but one that is free-draining. Gomphrenas should have a sunny position. Z9. *Propagation* Sow the seed in early spring under glass at 16–18°C (60–64°F), or sow directly into the soil where they are to grow in late spring.

Blue-flowered annuals

Ageratum houstonianum	*Limonium sinuatum* 'Blue
Borago officinalis	Bonnet'
Brachyscome iberidifolia	*Lobelia erinus*
Campanula medium	*Myosotis*
Centaurea cyanus	*Nemophila menziesii*
Consolida ambigua	*Nigella damascena*
Cynoglossum amabile	*Nigella hispanica*
Echium 'Blue Bedder'	*Nolana paradoxa* 'Blue
Gilia	Bird'
Lathyrus odoratus	*Salvia farinacea* 'Victoria'

Uses Gomphrenas have generally only been used as a bedding plant, but *G. dispersa* can be grown in hanging baskets and other containers. It can also be used in mixed borders. Gomphrena flowers are excellent for cutting and can also be dried.

Gomphrena globosa
This is the most commonly seen garden plant in the genus. It comes in a wide variety of colour, and there are an increasing number of varieties. Some, such as 'Q Formula Mixed', have mixed colours but are also issued as separate colours such as 'Q Lilac' or 'Q White'. 'Buddy' has deep purple flowers. It also has a smaller relative, 'Dwarf Buddy'. H 60cm (24in) S 30cm (12in).

Gomphrena 'Strawberry Fields'
This variety is one of the most widely available. It has bright red flower heads with tiny dots of yellow flowers showing between the brilliant bracts. It is taller than the above, reaching up to 75cm (30in) high.

Other plants Occasionally you may be able to find seed of other species, such as *G. dispersa* which is not such an upright plant. It has deep pink flowers.

GYPSOPHILA
Gypsophila
This large genus of more than 100 species provides us with a number of perennial and annual garden plants. They are characterized by their masses of tiny white or pink flowers, which float airily on thin wiry stems, looking almost like a puff of smoke or a cloud. These are beautiful plants and they should be grown more often, particularly since they fit into so many styles of gardening. H 60cm (24in) S 30cm (12in). **How to obtain** Gypsophila can sometimes be purchased as plants from garden centres and nurseries but a safer way of ensuring you get them is to order seed from one of the seed merchants. *Cultivation* Gypsophilas need a light, well-drained soil and a sunny position. Z5.

Propagation Sow the seed in the spring, in open ground where the plants are to flower. Alternatively, it can be sown under glass at 13–16°C (55–60°F) at the same time of year.
Uses Gypsophilas can be used in a variety of ways including in annual bedding borders and mixed borders, where they work especially well as edging. They can also be used in most containers. They make excellent cut flowers, especially for bouquets.

Gypsophila elegans
This is the main annual *Gypsophila* that is cultivated. It produces masses of flat, star-shaped flowers in white and pink. The species itself is beautiful, but there are also a number of cultivars, many with bigger flowers. 'Covent Garden' is a good cutting form with large white flowers. 'White Elephant' (a clumsy-sounding name for an elegant plant) has the largest white flowers. 'Giant White' is tall, with slightly smaller white flowers that are good for cutting. *G.e.* var. *rosea* has soft pink flowers while 'Bright Rose', 'Carminea' and 'Red Cloud' all have much darker pink flowers.

Other plants The other major annual is *G. muralis*. This is a dwarf gypsophila which is suitable for rock gardens, containers and edging. It has pink flowers with darker veins. There are several cultivars including the darker-flowered 'Gypsy'. 'Garden Bride' has white flowers.

Gypsophila elegans 'Covent Garden'

Helianthus annuus

Helichrysum bracteatum

Helichrysum petiolare

HELIANTHUS
Sunflower

This large genus is most famous for its giant sunflower, *H. annuus*. This is an annual but there are many more garden worthy plants which are perennials. *H. annuus* is the only annual in the genus, but it has many cultivars. Not all of these have large heads, but the largest can reach to over 30cm (12in) across and are packed with seeds arranged in wonderful patterns. The typical sunflower is a daisy with yellow outer petals and a yellow, orange or brown central disc. There are many variations on this, with the yellow being paler or darker, and some flowers even having red or brown petals. The height varies, but the tallest plants reach 3m (10ft) or more; some are double this. These plants flower from late summer into autumn.
How to obtain You can buy plants, but they are starved in small pots. It is best to raise your own from the widely available seed.
Cultivation Plant out once the danger of frosts has passed. To get really big flowers, enrich the soil with well-rotted organic material and keep it moist. Choose a sunny position and stake plants. Z7.
Propagation Sow the seed in individual pots in early spring at 16–18°C (60–64°F) under glass.
Uses Shorter ones can be used at the backs of mixed borders. Sunflowers can be grown as specimen plants or in a line to create a striking summer hedge.

They are good for children's gardens. Sunflowers are excellent for cutting and for producing bird seed.

Helianthus annuus 'Italian White'
True to its name, a plant with pale-coloured blooms.

Helianthus annuus 'Music Box'
This cultivar offers a mixture of colours including yellows, reds and browns and some bicolours. A short form. H 75cm (30in).

Helianthus annuus 'Moonwalker'
The flowers of this plant are a pale lemon-yellow. H 1.5m (5ft).

Helianthus annuus 'Prado Red'
This is a red form. It reaches 1.5m (5ft) in height.

Helianthus annuus 'Russian Giant'
This is a very tall variety, which is widely grown. It has large yellow flowers. Up to 4m (12ft).

Helianthus annuus 'Italian White'

Helianthus annuus 'Sunspot'
A dwarf variety, but with large flowers. H 60cm (24in).

Helianthus annuus 'Teddy Bear'
This plant produces relatively small flower heads but they are fully double and look quite furry. They are golden-yellow in colour. H 60cm (24in).

Helianthus annuus 'Velvet Queen'
This is another tall form, with striking red flowers. A beautiful plant. H 1.5m (5ft).

HELICHRYSUM
Helichrysum

A very large genus containing a mixture of annuals, shrubs and perennials. There are two species that are of particular interest to the annual gardener. *H. petiolare* is a shrub that is treated as an annual and grown for its foliage. The other is *H. bracteatum*. This is now called *Bracteantha bracteatum* but is still better known and

distributed under its older name so it is included here. This is primarily grown for its flower heads.
How to obtain The former is mainly bought as plants which are readily available, while the latter is usually purchased as seed.
Cultivation Helichrysums will grow in any well-drained garden soil. Z7.
Propagation Take cuttings of *H. petiolare* and overwinter the resulting plants under frost-free glass. Sow seed of *H. bracteatum* under glass in spring at 16–18°C (60–64°F).
Uses H. petiolare is excellent as a foliage plant anywhere in the garden but it is especially good for bedding and containers of all types. *H. bracteatum* is used for bedding. The flowers are good for cutting and drying.

Helichrysum bracteatum
This is an everlasting flower with daisy-like papery flower heads. The outer petals come in yellows,

Helichrysum 'Bright Bikini Mixed'

Helichrysum petiolare 'Goring Silver'

Hesperis matronalis var. albiflora

Hibiscus moscheutos

pinks, reds and white. The inner disc is yellow. Plants vary in height up to 1m (3ft) or more.

Bright Bikini is a series of bright doubles in red, pink, yellow or white. 'Frosted Sulphur' has pale yellow double flowers. 'Hot Bikini' is hot-red and orange. The King Size Series also have double flowers, with blooms that measure up to 10cm (4in) across and come in a variety of colours. 'Monstrosum' is another large double mixture, which is also available as single colours. 'Silvery Rose' is a particularly beautiful silvery rose-pink.

Helichrysum petiolare
This plant is grown for its silver foliage, and is particularly in demand for hanging baskets and other containers. H 50cm (20in)

HESPERIS
Sweet rocket
This genus contains about 30 species of perennials and biennials of which only a couple are of interest to annual gardeners. The main one is *H. matronalis*, which has been grown for centuries as a cottage-garden plant. It is actually a short-lived perennial but is usually treated as an annual or biennial. It is a member of the cabbage family, but has a beautiful sweet scent that fills the evening air. The lilac or white flowers seem to glow in the evening light. H 1m (3ft) S 45cm (18in).
How to obtain You occasionally find plants of the double forms, but the single forms are usually available only as seed.
Cultivation Any reasonable garden soil will suffice. They will grow in full sun or partial shade. Z6.
Propagation Sow the seed in the autumn or spring where the plants are to flower. It can also be sown in pots placed in an open frame. If the plants are allowed to remain in the ground until they shed their seed, they will self-sow. Double forms need to be raised from basal cuttings in spring.
Uses These plants can be used in bedding, but they are best employed in a mixed border, especially in an informal one.

Hesperis matronalis
This is the sweet rocket or dame's violet. The flowers are carried in loose heads in early summer. These flowers are either lilac or

S 1m (3ft). There are several cultivars including 'Variegatum' and 'Limelight, which has silvery lime-green leaves. 'Goring Silver' is a particularly fine silver form.

white (known as *H.m.* var. *albiflora*). Sometimes the lilac forms are deeper in colour, almost purple. The coloured flowers often become fused with white as they age. There are also double forms of the lilac, 'Lilacina Flore Pleno', and the white, 'Alba Plena'.

Other plants There is a very similar plant which is a biennial. This is *H. steveniana*. It is shorter and produces pale purple or white flowers. H 60cm (24in).

HIBISCUS
Hibiscus
This is a large genus of around 200 species of which only one or two annuals are grown in gardens, although several of the shrubs are often treated as such. The annual *H. trionum* is most commonly

grown. It is a spreading plant which carries a succession of attractive trumpet-shaped flowers up to 7cm (3in) across.
How to obtain Plants are rarely seen so it is best to obtain seed from seed merchants' catalogues.
Cultivation Plant out once the threat of late frosts has passed. Any reasonable garden soil will do but it must be well-drained. A sunny position is necessary. Z10.
Propagation Sow the seed in early spring at 16–18°C (60–64°F) under glass.
Uses Hibiscus are not suited to mass planting, but they are good in mixed borders. The spreading habit makes them excellent container plants.

Hibiscus trionum
The flowers are a beautiful cream colour which contrasts with a very dark purple central eye. H 75cm (30in) S 60cm (24in). There are several cultivars: 'Lyonia' is silvery-yellow while 'Sunnyday' has lemon flowers.

Other plants The annuals *Hibiscus cannabinus* and *H. radiatus* are sometimes offered as seed. They have creamy-white flowers, but red and purple forms are more commonly offered. Some shrubby hibiscus are occasionally used in warmer gardens in summer, being moved out from the conservatory or greenhouse in pots. They include *H. rosa-sinensis*, the Chinese hibiscus with its wealth of cultivars, and *H. moscheutos*.

Hesperis matronalis

Hibiscus trionum

Hordeum jubatum, with orange dahlias

HORDEUM
Barley

Although this genus contains about 20 species of grass, only one is generally grown in our gardens. This is *H. jubatum*, commonly known as squirrel tail grass. It is an annual or short-lived perennial. It has become almost a cult plant and can be seen in a wide range of elaborate bedding schemes. It is frequently bedded with seemingly unlikely partners, yet it often works. This is because it is a grass with a soft curving flower head that combines well with all kinds of plants, both flowering and foliage. The heads are pinkish-green in colour and in the sunlight they also have an attractive silvery, silky sheen. They turn straw-coloured as they age. H 50cm (20in) S 25cm (10in).

How to obtain Squirrel tail grass is occasionally available as plants. However, these are generally not worth buying as the plants are not happy in pots, and besides you need more than one or two plants for an effective display. It is much better to raise your own by sowing seed which is obtainable from a number of seed merchants and specialist societies.

Cultivation Any reasonable garden soil is suitable for hordeum. Like most grasses it needs a sunny position. Z5.

Propagation Sow the seed in spring in the open ground where the plants are to flower.

Uses Squirrel tail grass is best planted in drifts either in bedding displays or in mixed borders. If possible plant them where the sun will shine through the flower heads to show off their silkiness.

Other plants Hordeum hystrix is also sometimes offered, but it is difficult to find. It is similar to *H. jubatum*. *H. vulgare*, the cultivated barley, can also be grown. It is not as decorative as the above but it is still interesting and makes a good dried grass.

IBERIS
Candytuft

A genus of about 40 species of which several are frequently seen in gardens. This is another plant that belongs to the cabbage family, although you would be hard-pressed to see the resemblance unless you were a botanist. They are low-growing plants with flat or slightly domed heads of mainly white flowers, although there are also pink and reddish-purple forms. They have an old-fashioned look about them but they are still popular, partly because they can be used for a variety of purposes in the garden. They rarely reach more than 30cm (12in) high, often less, and they are frequently wider than they are tall.

How to obtain These are widely available as plants, either in bedding packs or as individual plants. If you want to raise your own plants, there are plenty of sources of seed.

Cultivation Plant or sow in any reasonable garden soil. Full sun is best; they can be placed in light shade, but they may grow leggy (produce long, bare stems). Z7.

Propagation Seed can be sown where it is to flower or it can be sown under glass at 13–16°C (55–60°F) in early spring.

Uses Candytufts can be used in any form of bedding scheme or as edging or as fillers in a mixed border. They can also be grown in containers. Candytufts are good plants for children's gardens because they are easy to grow and flower quickly.

Iberis amara

This is a taller form of candytuft with plants sometimes reaching up to 45cm (18in) but often less. The flower heads are possibly more domed than in other

Iberis crenata

species. They are mainly white, but there are also those that are flushed with purple. Another pleasing attribute is their attractive perfume.

There are a number of cultivars available, including 'Giant Hyacinth', 'Hyacinth Flowered', 'Iceberg', 'Snowbird' and the fragrant 'Pinnacle', all of which have white flowers.

Iberis umbellata

This is similar to the previous plant, except that there is more colour variation. As well as white there are pink, red and purple and lavender forms.

Most of the cultivars are sold in mixtures such as the Flash Series with its brightly coloured flowers, and the Fairy Series which produces flowers in softer shades. Some, however, are sold as separate colours. They include 'Flash White'.

Other plants I. crenata is a similar species to the above.

IONOPSIDIUM
Violet cress

This is a tiny genus of some five species of annual plants. Only one of them is grown to any extent and that not very frequently nowadays. This is *I. acaule*, which is variously known as violet cress or diamond flower. It is a charming low-growing plant with lilac, blue or white flowers. As it is a member of the cabbage family it has the usual four petals arranged in a cross. It flowers over a long period, from early summer well into the autumn, and is constantly covered in its star-like flowers. H 8cm (3in) high and slightly more in spread.

Iberis amara 'Giant Hyacinth'

Ionopsidium acaule

How to obtain Seed is not commonly available from most merchants so you will have to search for it, but the effort is very worthwhile. Plants are only rarely seen for sale.
Cultivation Violet cress will grow in any decent garden soil, although it should be moisture-retentive but at the same time free-draining. They should be planted in full sun. Z9.
Propagation Sow the seed in spring in open ground where the plants are to flower.
Uses This is a good plant for odd places, such as crevices in pavings or walls. More formally it can be used as edging in beds or for rock gardens. It can also be grown as a small pot plant, to be placed on a wall or at the front of a group of containers.

IPOMOEA
Morning glory
This is an enormous genus, providing plenty of variety for those who would like to explore it. There are more than 500 species, and many of them are climbers. There are a dozen or so in general cultivation, but probably more to come since the plants are becoming increasingly popular. Some are annuals but most are perennials which can either be grown in a conservatory or glasshouse, or grown as annuals and used outside in the summer. Being climbers they are particularly useful since there are not a great number of annuals that grow in this way. The flowers

are mainly trumpets; they are carried in the same way as those of convolvulus, to which morning glories are closely related. The main exception is *I. lobata*, which has spikes of narrow, almost tubular flowers. Morning glories

Ipomoea lobata

can grow up to 6m (20ft) in height, but when used as annuals they are more likely to reach only 2–3m (6–10ft).
How to obtain Morning glories are increasingly available as plants for use under glass. The true annuals are available as seed from most seed merchants.
Cultivation Plant out after the danger of frosts has passed in any reasonable, well-drained soil. A warm, sunny position is important. Supports are necessary. Z8–10.
Propagation Sow seed under glass in spring at 18–20°C (64–68°F). Germination is improved if the seed is soaked in warm water before being sown.
Uses Morning glories can be used anywhere in the garden where height and colour are required. This can be either in the open ground or in containers. They make good patio plants.

Ipomoea purpurea

Ipomoea lobata
This species is not quite so popular as it once was and so it is not offered so widely. However, it can still be found. It does not have the typical trumpet-shaped flowers but instead carries spikes of narrow flowers. These are orange-red in bud when they first open, but they gradually turn to cream as they age.

Ipomoea purpurea
The common morning glory is becoming increasingly popular. It carries purple trumpet-shaped flowers with white throats. It also has pink, white and striped cultivars. 'Milky Way' has white flowers with maroon stripes, while 'Scarlet O'Hara' is scarlet with a white throat.

Ipomoea tricolor
This is a very old favourite. It produces trumpets that are blue with a white eye. There are a few variations on this. 'Flying Saucers' produces blue and white flowers. 'Heavenly Blue' is still one of the most widely grown morning glories, with its sky-blue flowers and the ever-present white throat.

Other plants There are several other ipomoea species which are currently becoming increasingly popular. They include *I. coccinea*, *I. alba*, *I. × multifida*, *I. nil*, and *I. quamoclit*, all of which are well worth considering. They produce the typical trumpet-shaped flowers in a range of blues, purples and reds.

Isatis tinctoria

ISATIS
Woad

A genus of 30 plants that are mainly disregarded in the garden except for *I. tinctoria*. This was once used as a blue dye and it is still grown in herb gardens in memory of this. It is not in the frontline of decorative plants but it does produce masses of small yellow flowers on its tall upright stems in the summer. Once the flowering season is over, it is covered with masses of dangling black seed which can be very attractive, especially when they catch the sunlight. However, it will then self-sow. It probably doesn't deserve a place in borders but it fits well in wild-flower gardens where it produces a sunny display of colour. H 1.5m (5ft) S 45cm (18in).

How to obtain Woad is often available in plant form at specialist herb nurseries, but rarely elsewhere. However, seed is reasonably widely available.

Cultivation Any reasonable garden soil that is well-drained will be suitable. Woad should have a sunny position. It may need support in exposed sites. Z6.

Propagation Sow the seed in the spring where the plants are to flower. They will self-sow if left to set seed.

Uses Woad's main use is now confined to the herb garden, but it is a very good plant for wild-gardens. It would not look out of place in an informal setting, such as a cottage garden.

Other plants Just occasionally you may come across seed of *I. lusitanica* and *I. platyloba*, both of which are similar to, but shorter than, the above. Specialist societies are a good source of seed for these plants.

LABLAB
Lablab

Although this single species genus has been around in gardens for a long time it is only in relatively recent times that it has become more common. This is perhaps due to the attractive purple leaves of the main cultivar, 'Ruby Moon', which has become valued as a foliage plant. The species is *L. purpureus* which has previously been known as *Dolichos*. It is still sometimes found listed under this name in garden centres and catalogues. It is a member of the pea family and this is readily apparent from the pea-like flowers. They are big and carried in large numbers. Once flowering has finished, the plant produces large pods which provide another round of decoration. This plant has also inherited the tendency of the pea to climb, making it doubly valuable in the garden. It can get up to 6m (20ft) when grown as a perennial but as an annual it only reaches 2–3m (6–10ft) in an average summer.

How to obtain Lablab is now available in many garden centres as plants but the most reliable source is still seed which is available from most merchants.

Lablab purpureus (seed pods)

Cultivation Grow in any reasonable garden soil so long as it is free-draining. A position in full sun is required. Lablab needs some form of support to climb up. A tripod in a border is ideal, but it can be grown up any support, for example a pole or a wigwam of sticks. Z9.

Propagation Sow the seed of this plant under glass in spring at 21°C (70°F).

Uses Lablab is valuable for adding height to a mixed border or bedding scheme. The dark-leaved form is often used in more exotic plantings, where it mixes well with tropical plants.

Lablab purpureus

The flowers are pinkish-purple pea-like blooms that are tinged with paler pink. They are followed by deep purple, nearly black, seed pods. The foliage is green, tinged with purple.

The 'Ruby Moon' is more commonly seen than the species and is responsible for this plant's revival. This has a wonderful deep purple foliage which sets off both the flowers and the seed pods beautifully.

LANTANA
Lantana

This large genus of 150 shrubs and perennials includes a few plants that have been cultivated as plants for conservatories or glasshouses for some time, but they have also increasingly been grown as outdoor annuals. The main attraction is the superb flowers which are carried in domed or rounded heads. They come in several colours, and more excitingly they actually change colour so that the younger flowers at the centre are a different colour from than those on the margins. Thus they may be flamed-red around the perimeter of the head and gold, tinged with orange, in the middle. Be warned though, that however pretty these plants may look they do contain toxins which can have very unpleasant consequences if eaten.

In ideal conditions lantanas will grow up to 2m (6ft) in height and spread. However, as bedding plants they will get nowhere near this, reaching more like 60cm (24in) at most.

How to obtain Lantana are most commonly bought as plants, which are available either from garden centres or from specialist nurseries. However, the seeds are becoming more widely available, usually as mixtures.

Lablab purpureus

Lantana camara 'Snow White'

Lantana camara 'Radiation'

Lathyrus odoratus 'White Supreme'

A tumbling variety of *Lathyrus odoratus*

Cultivation Plant out only after the danger of frosts has passed, into a soil that is reasonably rich, but free-draining. Lantanas need a warm and sunny position. Z8.

Propagation Sow seed in spring under glass at 16–18°C (60–64°F). Take cuttings in summer and overwinter the young plants under glass.

Uses These make excellent bedding plants as well as being perfect for containers of all sorts.

Lantana camara

This is the main species that is available. It has a number of cultivars. Some are single colours such as 'Snow White' which is creamy-white rather than the pure white indicated by its name, but most are bicolours such as the amazingly bright red and orange of 'Radiation'. 'Cream Carpet' is another creamy-coloured one, while 'Mine D'Or' has lovely golden flowers. 'Feston Rose' is another bicolour with an unusual combination of pink and yellow blooms, and 'Schloss Ortenburg' is along the lines of 'Radiation' with red and orange flowers.

LATHYRUS
Pea

This is a very large genus of 150 species of which some are annuals. The best known of these is the sweet pea, *L. odoratus*, which is a climber. Traditionally it has been grown up some form over support and used in the border and for cutting. However, different forms have been bred so that there are now also low-growing ones for borders and trailing ones suitable for hanging baskets and other containers. They are prized for their colour and fragrance although the latter is missing from many modern varieties.

How to obtain Sweet peas are widely available both as plants, usually in multipacks, and as seed. There are several specialist merchants who offer large selections of sweet peas.

Cultivation Plant out in early spring into a rich soil that is free-draining. A sunny position is required. Supports are needed for most varieties. Z6.

Propagation Sow the seed in late winter at 16–18°C (60–64°F) under glass.

Uses These plants can be used for decorative purposes in borders or grown in separate beds or in the vegetable garden for cutting and for exhibition purposes. Shorter varieties can be used in all forms of containers.

Lathyrus odoratus

The species is a magnificent plant with smaller flowers than the cultivars. They come in bright purple and red and are highly scented. There are numerous cultivars, many aimed at gardeners who use them for cutting or exhibition. Most of the colours are much softer than the species, with soft pinks, blues and whites predominating. However, each year brighter reds and blues are introduced. Seed is most frequently sold as individual cultivars of one colour, such as the excellent 'White Supreme' or 'Jayne Amanda' which has rose-pink flowers. They are also widely sold as mixtures. Many are sold in groups, such as the Knee-hi Group, which are much shorter than usual.

Other plants There are other annual species such as the yellow *L. chloranthus* or the blue *L. sativus*.

Purple-flowered annuals

Antirrhinum 'Purple King'
Callistephus chinensis
Centaurea cyanus 'Black Ball'
Collinsia grandiflora
Eschscholzia californica 'Purple-Violet'
Eustoma grandiflora
Exacum affine
Heliotropium
Hesperis matronalis
Limonium sinuatum 'Midnight'
Limonium sinuatum 'Purple Monarch'
Lunaria annua
Papaver somniferum
Petunia
Salvia splendens 'Purple Beacon'

Lathyrus odoratus

Lathyrus sativus

Laurentia axillaris 'Blue Stars'

Lavatera trimestris 'Novella'

LAURENTIA
Laurentia

This group of plants is sometimes categorized as a separate genus, *Laurentia,* and sometimes included in *Isotoma.* It is a genus of nearly 20 species of which one is commonly grown as an annual, although it is a perennial. This is *L. axillaris.* It is a delightful plant that has come into recent prominence. It forms a rounded hummock of finely cut foliage. Above this are carried beautiful star-shaped flowers, which are up to 4cm (1½in) across. The plant can grow up to 60cm (24in) as a perennial but when grown as an annual it is usually about 25cm (10in) in height and about the same in spread.
How to obtain Laurentia is widely available as plants, sold in individual pots, from garden centres and nurseries, and also as seed from all the seed merchants. It may be sometimes found under the name *Isotoma.*
Cultivation Any reasonable garden soil will do but it must be free-draining. A sunny position is important. Z7.
Propagation Sow seed in the early spring under glass at 13–16°C (55–60°F). Cuttings can be taken in summer and the young plants overwintered under glass.
Uses This plant works very well in all areas of the garden. It can be used as bedding or in a mixed border. It is also an excellent choice for all forms of container, including hanging baskets.

Laurentia axillaris

It is doubtful whether the plants and seed under this name are the species; they are more likely to be the cultivar known as 'Blue Stars'. It has starry flowers that are a lovely blue in colour. They are produced in quantity over a long period. There is also a pink form called 'Pink Stars' or 'Starlight Pink', and occasionally you find white ones. They can now also be bought as mixtures.

Other plants There are a couple of other species which can occasionally be found. *L. anethifolia* has white flowers in the form 'White Stars'. *L. petraea* also has white flowers.

LAVATERA
Mallow

This is a genus containing about 25 species, of which some are perennials and shrubs and yet others are annuals. Of the last, one in particular is very widely grown. This is *L. trimestris,* which is prized for its showy funnel-shaped flowers. They are up to 12cm (4½in) across and are either glistening white or a striking pink. The pink forms often have a darker eye and radiating thin veins of darker pink. They are extremely good annuals, continuously covered in a profusion of blooms during the summer. H 1.2m (4ft) S 45cm (18in).
How to obtain Mallows can easily be found as plants in most garden centres. However, seed is also widely available from merchants, and usually offers a greater choice of cultivars.
Cultivation Plant out in any well-drained soil. Mallows must have a sunny position to do well. Z7.
Propagation Sow seed in the early spring under glass at 13–16°C (55–60°F). For later flowering, sow directly in the ground where the plants are to flower.
Uses Mallows make excellent bedding plants as well as being of great use in mixed borders. They can also be used in large tubs.

Lavatera trimestris

This species is rarely grown in its own right, but is often seen as one of its several cultivars. 'Silver Cups' is one of the best known. This has soft silvery-pink flowers, each with darker veins and a dollop of raspberry pink in the middle. 'Mont Blanc' is another favourite, with flowers of pure white. 'Pink Beauty' is very pale pink, with darker veins and central eye. 'Novella' is also pink.

Other plants Lavatera arborea is a biennial. While it is not in the same league as the above, it is excellent for wild-flower gardens, especially those on the coast or in sandy soils. The flowers are not as showy but they are the same funnel shape and come in a dull purply colour. This is a shrubby plant that can get quite tall. H 3m (10ft) when growing well.

LAYIA
Layia

You would be forgiven for thinking that this genus has only one plant, since that is all that most people know. In fact, there are 15 species of annual plants. The others have been grown in gardens in the past but their popularity has declined and now they are difficult to find. The one we still grow is *L. platyglossa.* It has also been known as *L. elegans* under which name it is still often sold. Its common name is tidy tips, which refers to the fact that the yellow petals have dainty white tips to them. The flowers are daisies up to 4cm (1½in) in diameter, with a ring of outer petals and an inner disc which is also yellow. The plants are upright. H 45cm (18in) S 30cm (12in). Some forms are more

Layia elegans

Limnanthes douglasii

sprawling and do not gain such a height, so they are better used in hanging baskets.

How to obtain Layias are getting more difficult to find, but some seed merchants still carry them in stock. Check under both species names.

Cultivation Any reasonable garden soil will suit these plants. Z7.

Propagation Sow the seed in spring in the open ground where the plants are to grow. They can also be sown in pots under glass at 13–16°C (55–60°F).

Uses Layia can be used as bedding or in mixed borders. They will also make a colourful addition to containers.

Other plants With determined searching, you may be able to find seed of *L. chrysanthemoides* since there is at least one merchant that still stocks it. This is a plant which carries bright yellow flowers. H 30cm (12in).

LIMNANTHES
Poached egg plant

This is one of those genera in which only one plant is generally grown, although there are up to 17 species from which to choose. The flowers look similar to those of *Layia* at first glance, although they are in no way related. *Limnanthes douglasii* is known as the poached egg plant because, as in *Layia platyglossa*, it has yellow petals with a white margin. In this case the petals are much broader and form a saucer shape. The plants

make wonderful edging to paths. They are particularly useful plants for dull days because they are so bright and cheerful they make it seem as if the sun is shining. Poached egg plants are much loved by bees. They are low-growing. They usually self-sow and can create a dense mat, making useful ground cover. H and S 20cm (8in).

How to obtain Poached egg plants are available as plants but they do not do well if confined in pots so it is best to sow your own seed. This is readily available. Once you have these plants they will produce copious amounts of seedlings, fortunately in the same area since they do not spread far.

Cultivation Any normal garden soil will do, but these plants should be positioned in the sun for the best effect. Z6.

Propagation Sow the seed where the plants are to flower in autumn or in spring.

Uses They make excellent bedding plants for the early summer, but can also be used as temporary fillers in mixed border. They are very good edging plants.

Limnanthes douglasii

This is nearly always grown as the species, described above. However, there is also a very rare variety known as *L.d.* var. *sulphurea* in which the white edging is missing, making the flowers all yellow.

Other plants Very occasionally, you may come across seed of *L. alba*. This is a white-flowered species which is similar to the above. However, it is not so attractive a plant since it is more sprawling and the flowers are smaller.

LINARIA
Toadflax

There are about 100 species in this genus which include perennials as well as annuals. Quite a large number of these annuals are grown in gardens, but they are not widely cultivated. This may be because they are grown mainly in mixed borders and have not really been developed for the bedding or container market. This also means that they are not so easy to find,

but the effort is worth it since there are some interesting plants out there. The one exception is *L. maroccana* which is facing a revival, with a number of cultivars now becoming available. Linarias vary in height from ground-hugging species to those that reach 75cm (30in) in height.

How to obtain Apart from that of *L. maroccana*, seed is difficult to find although it is available from some seed merchants and specialist societies. It is rare that you find any plants for sale.

Cultivation Any reasonable garden soil will be sufficient, but linarias prefer light soils that should be free-draining. Z6.

Propagation Sow the seed in spring in open ground where the plants are to flower.

Uses Linarias are good plants for the mixed border. *L. maroccana* can be used for bedding.

Linaria alpina

This species is strictly speaking a perennial but because it is short-lived, it is treated as an annual. It is a very low-growing plant. The small flowers are carried in short upright spikes and have a velvety texture. They are exquisite and are available in a wide range of purple-reds. Most are bicolours.

Linaria alpina is a very good plant for growing in crevices, between the cracks in paving and walls as well as on rock gardens. It self-sows without becoming a nuisance. H 8cm (3in).

Linaria maroccana 'Bunny Rabbits'

Linaria maroccana

The multi-coloured flowers are carried in spikes and look like miniature antirrhinums. H up to 45cm (18in). There are a few cultivars including Excelsior hybrids, 'Fairy Bouquet' and 'Northern Lights', all of which produce flowers in mixed colours of blue, purple, pink and yellow. 'White Pearl' is restricted to white flowers as its name suggests. 'Bunny Rabbits' bears white, pink and yellow blooms.

Linaria reticulata

These are tall plants with very attractive foliage and deep purple flowers, which are splashed with orange or yellow on the lower lip. H 1m (3ft). There is also a mixture, called 'Flamenco', now on offer.

Other plants *Linaria elegans* is a rather beautiful, tall plant that produces purple-pink flowers. It is well worth seeking out. H 70cm (28in).

Linaria maroccana 'Fairy Bouquet'

Lindheimera texana

LINDHEIMERA
Star daisy

Lindheimera texana is the only member of this genus and it has been popular in the garden for a long time. However, it now seems to be in decline since only a few seed merchants carry it. It is an upright plant, but is generally sturdy enough to stand without staking. The flowers are up to 2.5cm (1in) across and are carried in loose heads. They are yellow, varying from soft to golden hues, and comprising five petals arranged in a star shape. They appear in profusion over a long period through the summer. The yellow is set off perfectly by the bright green foliage and bracts that surround the flowers. H 60cm (24in) S 30cm (12in).

How to obtain The plants are not commonly sold, either in garden centres or nurseries, but the seed is offered by some merchants and occasionally by specialist societies in their seed exchanges. You will need to search for this plant.

Cultivation Plant out once the danger of frosts has passed. Star daisies will grow in any soil that is reasonably rich, but it should be well drained. A sunny position is required. Z8.

Propagation Sow the seed in early spring at 16–18°C (61–64°F) under glass.

Uses Star daisies can be used as bedding as they have a long flowering season, but they work equally well in a mixed border scheme, where a splash of bright yellow is required.

LINUM
Flax

A huge genus of 200 species which contains perennials as well as many annuals and biennials. The flaxes are characterized by their upward-facing, funnel-shaped flowers. Although generally thought of as blue, many have yellow or red flowers. There are a number of annuals for the keen gardener, but there is only one that is in widespread use. This is *L. grandiflorum*, which is a magnificent plant that is welcome in borders and bedding schemes alike. The perennial flaxes are short lived and can be used as annuals if their bright blue colour was desired. H up to 75cm (30in) S 15cm (6in).

How to obtain The seed of the main species, *L. grandiflorum*, is readily available but you will need

to search carefully for any other species. Plants are rarely, if ever, offered for sale.

Cultivation Flax should be grown in any reasonably fertile soil that is well-drained. They should have a sunny position. Z7.

Propagation Sow the seed in the open ground where the plants are to flower. Thin the seedlings to 15cm (6in) intervals.

Uses These plants can be used to create spectacular blocks of colour in a bedding scheme or planted as drifts in a mixed border.

Linum grandiflorum var. *rubrum*
This plant, which is often listed as a cultivar 'Rubrum', has brilliant red flowers with a dark eye; they are quite dazzling to look at. The variety *alba* has pure white flowers. The gem of this form is 'Bright Eyes' which has glistening white flowers with a crimson base to each petal and a black centre – they are stunning. There is another form, variously listed as *caeruleum* and 'Caeruleum', which has purplish-blue flowers.

Other plants Linum sulcatum is a rarely seen annual from Eastern USA. It has pale yellow flowers and grows to 75cm (30in) in height. It is worth growing if you can find seed.

Linum usitatissimum is the common agricultural flax. Its attractive blue flowers also make it an excellent garden plant. It works particularly well in a wild-flower garden where true

blue flowers are often lacking. There are some garden cultivars available, including 'Skyscraper'.

LOBELIA
Lobelia

This is an enormous genus of some 350 species. Most of those grown in the garden are perennials but there is one annual that is more popular then all of those put together. This is *L. erinus*. This is seen in all kinds of garden situations, from hanging baskets to rockeries and the edges of pathways. It must surely be one of the most useful and popular of all plants and has remained so for many generations.

The flowers are basically blue, with a white dot in the throat, but there are also pink, purple and red variations. It is a bushy, sprawling little plant which grows to about 25cm (10in) and a little more across. Some varieties produce an abundance of trailing stems which makes them useful in hanging baskets.

How to obtain Lobelia is widely sold in bedding packs and in individual pots by most garden centres. Seed is also widely sold and this is offered in a better choice of cultivars.

Cultivation Any good garden soil or potting compost (soil mix) will do for these plants. Lobelia is best planted in partial shade but it can be used in full sun so long as the soil does not dry out too much. Clip occasionally to keep the plants compact. Z7.

Linum grandiflorum var. *rubrum*

Lobelia erinus 'Cambridge Blue'

Propagation Sow seed in early spring under glass at 16–18°C (61–64°F). Plants may self-sow.
Uses Lobelia looks good anywhere. It is particularly useful in containers, where it often acts as a "filler", creating a background colour for other plants.

Lobelia erinus

The species is not grown as such; it is always cultivated as one of its many cultivars. The flower colour varies from blues, such as in the 'Cambridge Blue' with its sky blue flowers and the dark blue 'Crystal Palace', to cherry-red, as in 'Rosamund'. There are a number of series which are sold either as mixtures or as individual colours. The Cascade Series has trailing stems, and is excellent for hanging baskets. It includes 'Lilac Cascade' and 'Red Cascade'. Other Series include the Palace Series and Regatta Series.

LOBULARIA
Sweet alyssum

A small genus of five species from the Mediterranean area of which just one is grown in our gardens. This is sweet alyssum or sweet Alison, *L. maritima*. It is not a plant to set the world alight since it is not particularly showy. However, it is one of those plants that can act as a basic ingredient in the design of any garden. It is a perennial that is grown as an annual, although if left it may linger on in a somewhat straggly way for another year.

Sweet alyssum is low-growing, forming little hummocks of foliage which are covered with small white flowers for a very

Lobularia maritima 'Snow Crystals'

long period from summer into autumn. The flowers are sweetly scented (hence part of its name, the other part comes from the fact that the flower heads resemble those of *Alyssum*). They are carried in slightly domed heads. As well as the basic white there are cultivars that vary from pink to purple. H 5–30cm (2–12in) S up to 30cm (12in).
How to obtain These plants are frequently sold as bedding packs in most garden centres and many nurseries. Only a few of the cultivars may be available, but there should be no problem in getting white forms. For a bigger choice search the seed merchants' catalogues and grow your own.

Cultivation Any reasonable soil will do, so long as it is free-draining. It requires full sun. Z7.
Propagation Sow the seed in mid-spring in the open ground where the plants are to grow.
Uses Excellent for bedding schemes, especially where block or linear planting is required. Sweet alyssums can also be used as fillers or edging in mixed borders.

Lobularia maritima

The species is not often grown in its own right. It is more commonly found as one of its

cultivars. There are several series, including the Alice Series and Easter Bonnet Series, which produce a mixture of white, pink and purple flowers. There are also individual cultivars, including 'Snow Crystals' (white flowers), 'Snowcloth' (white), 'New Purple' (purple) or 'Navy Blue' (purple, not blue as one might assume from the name). There is also a variegated form called 'Variegata', which has pale green foliage edged with white. It may occasionally be found but this plant is not widely available.

Lobularia maritima 'Wonderland'

White-flowered annuals

Antirrhinum 'White Wonder'	*Iberis amara*
Argyranthemum frutescens	*Lathyrus odorata*
Clarkia pulchella 'Snowflake'	*Lavatera trimestris* 'Mont Blanc'
Cleome spinosa 'Helen Campbell'	*Lobelia erinus* 'Snowball'
Cosmos bipinnatus 'Sonata'	*Omphalodes linifolia*
Digitalis purpurea alba	*Osteospermum* 'Glistening White'
Gypsophila elegans 'Covent Garden'	*Pelargonium*
	Petunia

Lonas annua

LONAS
Lonas

This genus has one main species, *L. annua*, also known as the African daisy or yellow ageratum. This is yet another of those annuals that was once much more popular than it is now. Indeed although a number of seed merchants still list it in their catalogues it rarely crops in any literature about annuals. Its neglect is surprising because it is quite a showy plant and works well in borders. It is useful as a cut flower and can also be dried. The African daisy is a bushy plant with clusters of bright yellow flowers carried on reddish stems over a long period, lasting from midsummer through into the autumn. The flowers are prolific and they are also long-lasting which makes them very useful as bedding plants. H 30cm (12in) S 25cm (10in).

How to obtain Plants are very rarely seen on sale, but there are a large number of seed merchants offering lonas plants.

Cultivation Lonas will grow in any reasonable garden soil that is not too wet. It should be given a sunny position if possible. Z7.

Propagation Sow seed in early spring at 16–18°C (60–64°) under glass.

Uses Lonas makes an excellent bedding plant and can also be used to great effect in a mixed border or in containers.

Lonas inodora

The species is often grown in its own right, and there are also a couple of cultivars, 'Gold Rush' and 'Golden Yellow'. However, they are not a great deal different from the species.

LOTUS
Parrot's beak

This is a big genus containing about 150 species of shrubs and perennials. At least one of them is treated as an annual in the garden. This is *L. berthelotii*, a very beautiful plant for which everybody should be on the lookout. It is an evergreen shrub with prostrate stems. When the plant

Lotus berthelotii (foliage)

Lotus berthelotii (in flower)

is placed in a container such as a tall tub or a hanging basket, the stems hang over the edges to create curtains of foliage. The foliage is made up of narrow leaves carried in much the same way as those of lavender or rosemary. The great beauty of the leaves is that, again like those of the lavender, they are silver. This is a member of the pea family, and the relationship can be seen in the flowers. They are elongated and upward-curling, looking rather like a parrot's beak. They are scarlet and contrast beautifully with the cascades of silver foliage.

How to obtain Parrot's beak is widely available as plants, which are now carried by most garden centres as well as nurseries. It is sometimes offered as seed, but there is no advantage to be had from growing the plant from seed.

Cultivation In containers, use a loam-based potting compost (soil mix). If planted in an open garden, parrot's beak needs a free-draining soil. A sunny position is also necessary. Z8.

Propagation Take cuttings in summer from existing plants and overwinter the resulting plants under warm glass.

Uses The parrot's beak's main use is in containers from which the foliage can hang down. It can also be used in the garden, either on the flat where it can be used as bedding or on walls, down which the foliage can cascade.

Lotus berthelotii

This plant is most often grown as the species, described above. There is, however, some slight variation in colour, although this is not sufficient for cultivars to

Lunaria annua

LUNARIA
Honesty
A genus of one species, which is a biennial that is commonly grown. This tall plant was much loved by the Victorians and it is still very popular. In the spring it has striking purple flowers and these eventually produce oval seed pods; when their outer casings are discarded, they produce a silver disc which looks superb in dried flower arrangements. If you let some plants seed they will self-sow. H 1m (3ft), S 30cm (12in).
Cultivation Any garden soil will suffice and these plants will happily grow in shade or sun. Z8.
Propagation Honesty can be propagated simply by sowing the seed where you want the plants to grow. A small plant is produced in the first year and flowering is in the following spring.
Uses Honesty is good for mixed borders and informal plantings among shrubs or trees.

Lunaria annua
This is the only species that is worth growing. The species has purple flowers but there is also a most beautiful white variety, *albiflora*. There are several variegated forms including 'Variegata', with purple flowers and white marginal variegations to the leaves, and a white-flowered form called 'Alba Variegata'. 'Munstead Purple' has darker purple flowers.

Malcolmia maritima

MALCOLMIA
Virginia stock
Of the 35 species in this genus only one, *Malcolmia* (sometimes confusingly spelt *Malcomia*) *maritima*, is in general cultivation. It is pretty little annual which is still managing to hold on to its popularity in spite of there being many showier plants around. Its thin stems are smothered with small, four-petalled flowers from spring right through into autumn. These are white, pink or purple with a white eye. Unlike the larger stocks to which it is related, this plant has no scent. Virginia stocks have an old-fashioned, prettiness, and they are ideal for bedding or for filling gaps in the mixed border. There were once several cultivars of the species, including white forms, but these are no longer sold. H 38cm (15in) S 15cm (6in).

How to obtain Virginia stocks are sometimes sold as plants. The seed is readily available.
Cultivation Sow in any reasonable garden soil, preferably one that is free-draining. Virginia stocks need a sunny position. Z7.
Propagation Sow in spring, in the open ground where the plants are to flower. If allowed to set seed they will self-sow.
Uses These plants look good in drifts, as bedding or in a mixed border. They are also good for edging paths and ideal for children's gardens, since they are easy to grow, quick to flower and stay colourful over a long period.

Other plants M. *flexuosa* is similar to the above, M. *bicolor* has pink or yellow flowers, and M. *littorea* has large purple-pink ones. You may be able to find these offered by specialist societies.

be delineated. Some flowers contain more orange, making them a flame colour, while others are a darker red. You will need to see the plants in flower if you wish to buy one of these variants.

Other plants The only other plant worth mentioning is sometimes called *L. tetragonolobus* and sometimes *Tetragonolobus purpureus*. This is the asparagus pea, which has edible pods but can be grown as a decorative plant. It is a low-growing annual with stems that grow up to 40cm (16in). It has small pea-like flowers. They are an attractive bright red, which contrasts well with the foliage.

Lunaria annua var. albiflora

Yellow-flowered annuals

Alcea rosea 'Yellow'	*Limonium sinuatum*
Anoda cristata	'Forever Moonlight'
'Buttercup'	*Limnanthes douglasii*
Argemone mexicana	*Lonas annua*
Argyranthemum frutescens	*Mentzelia lindleyi*
'Jamaica Primrose'	*Mimulus*
Chrysanthemum segetum	*Sanvitalia procumbens*
Coreopsis 'Sunray'	*Tagetes erecta*
Glaucium flavum	*Tagetes patula*
Helianthus annuus	*Tropaeolum peregrinum*

Malope trifida

Matthiola longipetala subsp. *bicornis*

Matthiola Brompton Stock

MALOPE
Annual mallow

This is a small genus of four species, but only one annual is in general cultivation. Even this is less popular than it once was, but happily it is still available to those who want an attractive but not too commonly seen plant. The plant in question is *M. trifida*. The mallow part of the name comes from the fact that the flowers resemble those of the mallow (to which it is related). These are funnel- or trumpet-shaped and up to 8cm (3in) across. Their colour is purple-red, with deeper purple veins running into the centre. They appear over a long period from summer well into autumn, and contrast beautifully with the green foliage. H 1.5m (5ft) S 30cm (12in).

How to obtain Annual mallows are occasionally available as plants from garden centres and nurseries, but don't rely on finding them. It is better to obtain seed from one of the seed merchants.

Cultivation These plants will grow in virtually any reasonable garden soil so long as it is free-draining. A sunny position is best but they will grow in a little shade. Z7.

Propagation Sow the seed into open ground in spring where they are to flower or sow under glass in early spring at 13–16°C (55–60°F).

Uses Like most mallows, these are excellent for coastal gardens. They also make very attractive cut flowers.

Malope trifida

The species, described above, is grown in its own right, and there are also a few cultivars available. One of the best of these is 'White Queen', which, as its name suggests, has white flowers. 'Pink Queen' (pink flowers) and 'Red Queen' (red flowers) are also available. One of the newer cultivars is a mixture called 'Glacier Fruits' which includes pink, red and white blooms, as does 'Crown Mix'. 'Vulcan' is a larger plant which carries deep purplish-red flowers.

MATTHIOLA
Stock

This is a medium-sized genus of some 55 species of which a number are annuals or biennials. Among them are some of the best annuals for the garden. Their attraction lies partly in their magnificent compact flower heads, which come in a variety of bright or soft colours, and partly in their powerful scent. Their popularity is reflected in the fact that seed merchants sell a large range of varieties and frequently offer new ones. Looking at the dense spikes of flowers it is hard to imagine that these plants are in the cabbage family. The range of colours includes the cabbage's yellow, but generally the flowers come in a wide range of pinks, purples and reds as well as white. They are quite large, up to 2.5cm (1in) across. The scent is sweet and mainly occurs in the evening. H 60cm (24in) in some varieties, S 30cm (12in) across.

How to obtain Stocks are widely available as plants, and garden centres and nurseries sell them in packs as well as in individual pots.

Matthiola incana 'Legacy Mixed'

A larger range of varieties is available in seed form from the various merchants.

Cultivation Generally these plants are happy in any reasonable garden soil, with the usual proviso that it should be free-draining. A warm sunny position is also necessary. Z6.

Propagation Most can be sown in early spring under glass at 13–16°C (55–60°F). The night-scented stock can be sown in spring in the open ground where the plants are to flower.

Uses Stocks make excellent bedding material, but they can also be planted as drifts in a mixed border. They can also be used in containers. Site the sweetly scented ones on patios or near to sitting areas. Stocks make excellent cut flowers.

Matthiola incana

This is an upright, shrubby plant with greyish-green foliage. The dense heads of flowers come in white, or shades of pink, red or purple. The plants are generally sold in two main groups: the Brompton stocks, which are biennial, and the ten-week stocks, which are annual. The flowers are either single or double.

There are plenty of varieties of both; available either as mixtures or in single colours. Among them is the Cinderella Series, whose plants grow up to 30cm (12in) high, bearing well-scented double flowers in colours that include lavender and blue. 'Legacy Mixed' are also doubles but they are taller. The Midget Series are just 25cm (10in) high; the flowers come in a wide range of colours.

Matthiola longipetala subsp. *bicornis*

This is the very charming night-scented stock which produces loose heads of single flowers that are sweetly scented at night. They are especially good for planting beneath bedrooms. There are several varieties available, and these include 'Evening Fragrance' and 'Starlight Scentsation'. H 35cm (14in) S 23cm (9in).

MELIANTHUS
Honey bush

Not many annuals are used purely for foliage purposes, but *M. major* is one such plant. It is, in fact, a perennial shrub and not an annual at all, but it is usually treated in this way in gardens. It is one of a genus of six shrubby species. The great feature about it is the large leaves which are pinnate (arranged as leaflets on either side of the main leaf stalk). The foliage is a blue- or grey-green and the leaves are noticeably toothed, both features adding to the overall visual effect. In warmer areas, this plant can be treated as a perennial and kept for several years in which case it can become quite big, up to 3m (10ft) tall. As an annual, its height is about 1m (3ft) or so and the same across. If kept more than one year there is also the possibility that it will flower. The blooms are red and are produced in tall spikes.

How to obtain Available both as plants from garden centres and as seed, although the latter are becoming difficult to find since some of the major seed merchants have stopped stocking it.

Melianthus major

Cultivation Honey bushes will grow in any fertile garden soil that is moisture-retentive but at the same time free-draining. They should be planted in a sunny position. Z9.

Propagation Sow seed in early spring under glass at 13–16°C (55–60°F).

Uses This plant can be used in many places in the garden. It is attractive in its own right and can also be used as a foil to other plants. It works well as bedding but its main use is as small plantings in either mixed borders or containers.

Other plants Although *M. major* is declining in availability, other species are becoming more available if you are prepared to search for them. *M. minor* is a smaller, downy version of the above. *M. comosus*, *M. pectinatus* and *M. villosus* are sometimes available.

MENTZELIA
Starflower

This is a large genus containing some 60 species of which *M. lindleyi* is the only one generally grown. Name changes have bedevilled annuals and this is another of those that has altered. Until recently it was known as *Bartonia aurea*, under which name it is still often sold. Its attraction is the golden-yellow flowers which are flushed red at their base and produced over a long period. Each flower has five rounded petals, each of which are pointed at their

tip, giving them their star-like quality. The flowers are quite large, up to about 5cm (2in) in diameter, and they produce a wonderful scent in the evening. The golden-yellow is set off beautifully by the green foliage which is finely cut. H 45cm (18in) S 25cm (10in).

How to obtain Starflowers are rarely available as plants but the seed is offered by a number of seed merchants. It is often listed under the name *Bartonia*.

Cultivation Any reasonable garden soil will be suitable for star-flowers, so long as it is free draining. These plants require a sunny position. Z9.

Propagation Sow the seed in early spring in open ground where the plants are to flower.

Uses Starflowers make excellent bedding and they can also be used successfully in a mixed border. It is also worth experimenting with them as container plants. They are best planted in a site where their evening fragrance can be appreciated, such as under the windows of living areas.

Other plants A few of the other species are occasionally grown but you will have to search to find them. *M. laevicaulis* is a biennial producing pale yellow flowers that open to twice the size of the above. It is very attractive and deserves to be more widely known. *M. involucrata* is another, this time with creamy-coloured flowers that have a satin-like texture. The flower centres are tinged with crimson. It is worth looking for among the specialist society lists.

Mentzelia lindleyi

Orange-flowered annuals

Antirrhinum majus 'Sonnet Orange Scarlet'	*Mimulus* 'Malibu'
Calceolaria 'Sunset Mixed'	*Nemesia* 'Orange Prince'
Calendula officinalis	*Papaver nudicaule*
Celosia cristata 'Apricot Brandy'	*Rudbeckia hirta*
Erysimum 'Orange Bedder'	*Tagetes erecta*
Eschscholzia californica	*Tagetes patula*
Helichrysum bracteatum	*Thunbergia alata*
	Tithonia rotundifolia 'Torch'
	Tropaeolum majus
	Zinnia haageana 'Orange'

Moluccella laevis

MOLUCCELLA
Bells of Ireland

Moluccella is a small genus of four species, of which *M. laevis* is by far the best known by gardeners. This is the famous bells of Ireland or shell flower. The second name is quite apt because the flowers do indeed look like shells. They are very small, each one cupped in a cone-shaped green bract, which gives it its shell-like appearance. The flowers are white or pale purple and they are fragrant. They are carried in upright spikes with the cones facing outward, looking rather like a modern radio mast covered with dishes. Despite its name, this plant has little to do with Ireland. In fact, it is a native plant of south-west Asia, found growing in countries such as Turkey and Iraq. H 1m (3ft) S 25cm (10in).
How to obtain This plant is normally grown from seed which is generally available from most seed merchants. The rare *M. spinosa* is very difficult to find but it is worth checking specialist society seed lists, which sometimes offer it.
Cultivation Bells of Ireland will grow in any free-draining garden soil. They must have a sunny position. Z8.
Propagation Sow seed in late spring in open ground where the plants are to flower. For earlier flowering, raise plants under glass by sowing in early spring at 13–16°C (55–60°F).

Uses This plant can be used in a variety of positions in the garden, including as bedding or in mixed borders. It makes a good cut flower and is excellent for drying.

Other plants If you are lucky, you may be able to track down *M. spinosa*. This is a pretty plant in which the white flowers are also set in cups but this time they are tipped with spines. It has red stems and is quite tall, so it needs a position at the back of a border. H 2m (6ft) S 30cm (12in).

MYOSOTIS
Forget-me-nots

This is a genus of plants that is familiar to most gardeners. The sky-blue flowers seem to have been designed to lift the spirits as winter departs and spring takes over. Several of the 50 species are in cultivation, although not all of them are annuals. They are generally small, clump-forming plants. The small flowers are carried in spikes that gradually unroll, getting longer. There are usually three stages of flowers present in each spike: seed at the bottom, open flowers above them and buds in the opening coil. The flowers come in shades of blue and have yellow centres, but there are also a few cultivars producing blooms in white and pink. H and S 30cm (12in).
How to obtain Forget-me-nots can be bought as plants, but they do not do brilliantly unless they are transplanted when young. Seed is a better bet and fortunately it is widely available.
Cultivation Any reasonable garden soil will be sufficient. Plant in full sun; these plants will also grow in shade, but will become somewhat leggy (producing long, bare stems). Remove after flowering to prevent excessive self-sowing. Z5.
Propagation Sow the seed in the open ground where the plants are to flower. Sow in summer for spring flowering and spring for summer flowering. Most plants will self-sow so there is no need to propagate after the first season.
Uses Forget-me-nots weave between and under other plants, making them perfect for mass carpeting. They can be used either

Myosotis sylvestris

in a bedding scheme – they are traditionally associated with tulips – or in a mixed scheme.

Myosotis sylvestris
This is the forget-me-not most often seen. It is usually a biennial but can be a short-lived perennial. It usually reaches 30cm (12in) in height but some forms are much less. The species has sky-blue flowers but there are cultivars with pink or white blooms. Some are sold as mixtures, such as Ball Series. This can also be obtained in single colours, including 'Snowball' (white). The Victoria Series contains 'Victoria Rose', which has rose-pink flowers. It is one of the shortest forget-me-nots, reaching a height of only 10cm (4in).

Other plants *Myosotis alpestris* is a short-lived perennial which can also be used as an annual. It produces dense heads of typical blue flowers. If you can find it *Cryptantha intermedia* is an interesting plant. Although it is not related to the forget-me-not, it looks very similar to it. It comes in white, and there are also orange and yellow variants, which look good mixed in with the true forget-me-not.

NEMESIA
Nemesia

This is a genus of about 50 species. It provides us with one of the annuals most frequently seen in the garden, *N. strumosa*. The flowers are numerous and produced over a long period. They

Nemesia strumosa 'KLM'

are about 2.5cm (1in) across and look like snapdragons, except that the bottom lip is flat and not inflated. There is a big colour range, including white, pink, red, purple, blue and yellow; there are often several flower colours mixed in one plant. H 15–30cm (6–12in) S 15cm (6in) or more.

How to obtain Nemesias are widely available in bedding packs as plants, but a greater range of options is available as seed.

Cultivation Any reasonable garden soil is suitable so long as it does not dry out completely. A sunny position is needed. In containers use a general potting compost (soil mix), preferably a loam-based one. Z9.

Propagation Sow seed in early spring under glass at 13–16°C (55–60°F).

Uses Nemesias are widely used in bedding schemes as well as for filling in gaps in mixed borders. They also suitable for containers of all types.

Nemesia strumosa

This is the main plant of the genus. It is not often sold as the species; it is much more likely to be found as one of the many varieties that are available. These include series, such as Carnival Series, and individual varieties, such as 'Danish Flag' with its red and white flowers, and 'KLM' with its blue and white blooms.

NEMOPHILA
Nemophila

A couple of unassuming and yet popular annuals belong to this genus of about 11 species. The

Nemophila menziesii

flowers are not remarkable but somehow they manage to catch the attention in a quiet way. They are saucer-shaped with five white petals, the tip of each having a coloured spot which is generally blue. Nemophilas flower over a long period in the summer, lasting into the autumn. The plants are fairly small. H and S about 30cm (12in) in the taller cultivars.

How to obtain Nemophilas can be purchased as plants, in bedding packs, at the majority of garden centres and nurseries. They are also widely available as seed from most seed merchants.

Cultivation Nemophilas can be grown in any free-draining garden soil. A good potting compost (soil mix) should be used for container plants. Do not let the soil dry out too much, either in the ground or in the containers, especially during very hot weather. A sunny position is best although these plants will tolerate a little shade. Z8.

Propagation The seed can be sown in spring directly into the soil where the plants are to flower. You can also sow them under glass at 13–16°C (55–60°F).

Uses The spreading nature of these plants mean that they are ideal for use in containers, especially hanging baskets and window boxes. They also make good bedding plants as well as being suitable for filling gaps in the mixed border and making good edgings to borders and beds.

Nemophila maculata

This plant is commonly known as five spot, and is the taller of the two species grown. *Nemophila maculata* is not seen quite so frequently as *Nemophila menziesii*, mainly because it has no cultivars. The flowers measure up to 4cm (1½in) across and have white petals with violet-blue spots.

Nemophila menziesii

This is popularly known as baby blue eyes. True to its name, it has blue flowers with white centres but there are some varieties that have pure white flowers. 'Penny Black' is the most startling of all the varieties since it has black flowers that are edged with white. 'Oculata' has pale blue flowers with a deep purple eye.

Nemophila maculata

Nemesia strumosa

Nicandra physalodes

NICANDRA
Shoo-fly flower

This is a single species genus with *N. physalodes* being the only member. It is commonly called the shoo-fly flower, presumably because of its ability to keep flies at bay. It is quite a spectacular plant when well grown since it is tall and has spreading branches. The flowers are funnel-shaped. They come in pale lilac-blue and have white centres. Individually they are not long lived, but a constant succession of them is produced from midsummer right through to the first frosts. The flowers are followed by round fruits (which give this plant its other name of apple of Peru). These then split open to reveal hundreds of seeds, which tend to self-sow with gay abandon. H 1.2m (4ft) S 1m (3ft)

How to obtain Shoo-fly flowers are rarely seen as plants because they do not do well when confined to small pots. However, it is possible to find seed since several seed merchants carry it.

Cultivation Any reasonable garden soil will do, but the plants will do best if it is enriched with plenty of well-rotted organic material. They need a sunny position. Z8.

Propagation Shoo-fly flowers come readily from seed. It should be sown in spring, directly in the soil where the plants are to flower. After the first year the plants will self-sow.

Uses These are best used as structural plants in a mixed border. They could also look quite spectacular in an imaginative bedding scheme. They can be grown in a large container, such as a tub or pot.

Nicandra physalodes

The species, described above, is grown in its own right. There is also one cultivar, namely 'Violacea'. This has darker flowers and inflated calyces which hold the flowers. These are flushed with a purple so dark it is almost black, and add to the plant's attraction.

NICOTIANA
Tobacco plant

This is a large genus of about 70 species of which a few are grown widely in our gardens. *N. alata* has long been a popular bedding plant as has its hybrid *N. × sanderae* under which name most of the cultivars are collected. *N. sylvestris* has been around for a long time but it is relatively recently that this tall plant has become so popular. The tobacco plants all have tubular flowers that flare out like trumpets. They come in a wide range of colours. Some have a wonderful scent, which is most noticeable in the evening. They tend to be long lasting, from summer well into the autumn.

How to obtain Plants are sold in bedding packs in all garden centres and many nurseries. However, a bigger range of plants can be obtained by growing them from seed which is readily available.

Cultivation Nicotiana will grow in any reasonable garden soil. If it is relatively dry or well-drained, overwinter them – many plants survive into a second year. They prefer a sunny position although they will grow in light shade. Z7.

Propagation Sow the seed in early spring under glass at 16–18°C (55–60°F).

Uses These are excellent for bedding schemes as well as being useful in mixed borders. The shorter varieties can also be used in containers.

Nicotiana sylvestris

Nicotiana alata

This plant used to be known as *N. affinis* and you will still sometimes see it being sold as such. This is a tall plant, with flowers that are pale green on the outside and white on the inside. The flowers are also fragrant. A good plant for mixed borders. H 1m (3ft).

Nicotiana 'Lime Green'

This plant is shorter than the above, reaching 60cm (24in). It has large lime-green blooms.

Nicotiana × sanderae

A range of garden hybrids with flowers in various colours,

Nicotiana 'Lime Green'

Nicotiana langsdorffii

Nigella damascena 'Miss Jekyll'

including pink and red. There are several series including the popular Domino Series, whose plants have a wide range of colours; single-coloured plants such as 'Domino Salmon Pink' are also available. This is one of the taller forms, reaching 45cm (18in) in height.

Nicotiana sylvestris
A tall species, good for the back of the border. It carries a loose head of long-tubed, white flowers, which are scented. H 2m (6ft).

Other plants *Nicotiana langsdorffii* has long, pendant flowers with a small flare at the mouth. They are lime-green. The plant used for tobacco and snuff, *N. tabacum*, has white and red flowers.

NIGELLA
Love-in-a-mist
This is a much loved genus of 20 annuals, of which a couple are regularly grown in our gardens. The flowers are really delightful. They are discs of blue with a prominent central boss, and are surrounded by a ruff of very finely cut leaves. Each flower looks rather like an exquisite brooch. There are also white and pink forms. Once the flowers are over, they produce an oval, inflated seed case, still surrounded by the filigree leaves. These plants have a wonderful old-fashioned quality and so make an ideal choice for a cottage garden. H 60cm (24in) S 25cm (10in).
How to obtain Nigellas can be seen for sale as plants, but these rarely come to much. It is a much better option to buy seed, which is readily available.
Cultivation Any reasonable garden soil should be perfectly suitable. Nigellas tend to prefer a position in full sun but some do well in the shade. Z7.
Propagation Sow the seed in autumn or spring in the open ground where the plants are to flower. They will self-sow if left to shed their seed.
Uses These plants can be used in bedding or in mixed borders. It is a good idea to allow them to self-sow so that the plants are dotted around.

Nigella damascena
The true species has single flowers but most of those grown in the garden are a mixture of single or semi-double blooms. In the wild the flowers are pale blue. This is the most frequently seen colour in gardens but cultivars are also available in pink, violet-blue and white. 'Miss Jekyll' has soft blue flowers. The Persian Jewel Series is a mixture of colours. 'Mulberry Rose' is pink while 'Dwarf Moody Blue' is a tiny variety only 20cm (8in) high.

Other plants *Nigella hispanica* and its cultivars are similar to *damascena*.

Nigella damascena 'Persian Jewel'

Annuals with good foliage

Amaranthus caudatus	Ocimum basilicum
Atriplex hortensis 'Rubra'	'Purple Ruffles'
Bassia scoparia	Onopordum acanthium
trichophylla	Pelargonium
Beta vulgaris	Perilla frutescens
Brassica oleracea	Plectranthus
Canna	Ricinus communis
Euphorbia marginata	Senecio cinerarea
Galactites tomentosa	Silybum marianum
Helichrysum petiolare	Tropaeolum majus 'Alaska'
Melianthus major	Zea mays

Nolana paradoxa

Oenothera biennis 'Wedding Bells'

NOLANA
Nolana

This is a genus containing some 18 species, of which a couple are grown in the garden. Nolana is one of those plants that is attractive without being showy. It is not in the top league for popularity and yet it still goes on selling. The plants are low growing and make an excellent carpet of flowers during the summer. Nolanas are covered with masses of trumpet-shaped flowers. These are upward-facing so it is easy to see past their colourful bells into the throats. H 25cm (10in) S 50cm (20in).

How to obtain Nolanas are occasionally found as plants in garden centres but if you want to be sure of getting them, obtain seed from seed merchants. This is readily available.

Cultivation Nolanas will grow in any reasonable garden soil, so long as it is free-draining. They need to be planted in a sunny position. Z10.

Propagation Sow the seed in early spring under glass at 13–16°C (55–60°F). For later flowering, nolanas can also be sown in spring directly into the soil where the plants are to flower.

Uses They make excellent bedding plants and can also be used for filling gaps in a mixed border. Nolanas make good plants for edging a bed or border. Their spreading nature also makes them a natural choice for hanging baskets, window boxes and other forms of container.

Nolana humifusa

This plant is usually seen as one of its various cultivars. 'Little Bells' has lilac flowers with streaks on its white throat. 'Shooting Stars' also has lilac flowers but this time they have a dark purple eye and streaks. In both, the flowers are about 2.5cm (1in) across. The plants have quite a wide spread, which makes them an excellent choice for hanging baskets. H 15cm (6in) high S 45cm (18in).

Nolana paradoxa

This charming species produces flowers of deep blue, with the blue fading into a white throat and yellow eye. They are slighlty taller than the previous plant. H 25cm (10in).

The cultivar 'Blue Bird' has deep blue flowers while 'Snowbird' has pure white flowers and the same yellow eye.

Other plants The plant once known as *N. lanceolata*, now *N. paradoxa* subsp. *atriplicifolia*, has silvery-haired leaves and sky-blue flowers.

NONEA
Nonea

This is one of the rarer annuals. It is not seen very often but can be found. In fact, as the author began to write this piece, a seed list arrived in the post in which offers included the very rare (in gardening terms) *N. rusica*. Although none of the 35 species is common, *N. lutea* is the plant most commonly seen. It will undoubtedly be of great interest to those who love the perennial pulmonarias as it offers them a very similar annual form. One important difference is that this plant has yellow flowers, a colour that is missing among pulmonarias. It flowers in spring. H 60cm (24in) S 25cm (10in).

Nonea lutea

How to obtain Plants and seed are very rare, though seed is slightly more common, sold mainly by specialist societies.

Cultivation Plant in moist, woodland-type soil, and ideally in light-dappled shade, although sun will be tolerated if the soil is kept moist enough. Z7.

Propagation Sow fresh seed in summer in pots and place in a shaded open frame without heat.

Uses Plant in spring bedding or, to best effect, in an informal woodland setting or shady border.

Nonea lutea

This is sometimes called yellow monkswort. The leaves are bristly and rather coarse. The flowers are small funnels of primrose-yellow. They appear in the spring.

Other plants Although rare, *N. pulla* is sometimes offered. It has deep purple flowers. *N. rusica* can also occasionally be found.

OENOTHERA
Evening primrose

This beautiful genus has 125 species, of which a surprising number are grown in gardens. The majority are perennials but many of these are short lived and can be thought of as annuals. There are also one or two that are true annuals or biennials. Of these, *O. biennis* is by far the most common, although it is not necessarily the most beautiful. Evening primroses are so-called because their flowers open mainly in the evening.

The flowers only last a day but there are usually plenty of buds waiting to open, which ensures a constant supply of blooms. Many of the forms in cultivation also open during the day, and some have a fine fragrance. They vary in height considerably.

How to obtain The best way to obtain these plants is from seed which is reasonably easy to find. Specialist societies offer the widest range. Plants are sometimes seen, but evening primroses do not do well if confined to small pots and so the results are often disappointing.

Cultivation Any reasonable garden soil will suffice, so long as it is free-draining. A warm, sunny position is required for these plants. Z4.

Propagation Seed can either be sown in the open ground where the plants are to flower or it can be sown in pots under glass at 13–16°C (55–60°F). Some species, *O. biennis* in particular, self-sow prodigiously.

Uses Evening primroses are mainly used in a mixed border, especially in informal plantings where they can be left to self-sow.

Oenothera biennis

This is a tall plant that produces masses of lemon-yellow flowers throughout the summer and autumn. It self-sows heavily so remove plants before too much is scattered. H 1.5m (5ft) S 60cm (24in). The cultivar 'Wedding Bells' has white flowers with yellow centres.

Oenothera deltoides

This is the desert evening primrose and as its name suggests it needs very sharp drainage. It has beautiful, glistening white flowers that fade to pink. They are up to 8cm (3in) across. H 30cm (12in) S 25cm (10in).

Oenothera glazioviana

This evening primrose produces lemon-yellow flowers, and is very similar to *O. biennis*.

Oenothera pallida

This plant is a beautiful white-flowered form whose blooms turn to pink as they age.

There is also a cultivar available, which is called 'Innocence'. H and S 50cm (20in).

Other plants The perennial species *Oenothera fruticosa* and *O. stricta* can be used as annuals.

OMPHALODES
Navelwort

This is a medium-sized genus containing about 28 species of which a number of perennials are grown in the garden. There is also one rather beautiful annual, *O. linifolia*. This seems to be one of those "secret" annuals; it is widely grown by those who know about it but not many gardeners do seem to know it. It is a delightful plant with powdery blue-green leaves on an upright, branching plant. The flowers are white and closely resemble the shape and size of forget-me-nots. The whole plant has a light and airy look to it. It self-sows and so once you have it, it rarely deserts you. H 30cm (12in) S 15cm (6in).

How to obtain Occasionally you see navelworts offered as plants, but these rarely do well when planted out. It is best to grow your own plants from seed, which is not too difficult to find.

Cultivation Any reasonable garden soil is sufficient so long as it is free-draining. A sunny position is required. Z7.

Propagation Sow the seed in spring in the open ground where the plants are to flower. If left to set seed they will self-sow, without becoming a nuisance.

Omphalodes linifolia

Uses *O. linifolia* is a delightful annual for growing in gaps in a mixed border. It is perfect for a white-themed garden or border.

Other plants As well as *Omphalodes linifolia*, which is described above, other annuals you may find include *O. brassicifolia* and *O. littoralis*. They are both quite rare but they have the same attractive white flowers, so it is worth looking out for them.

ONOPORDUM
Scotch thistle

Now we come to one of the giants of the annual world – the Scotch thistle. There are just a couple of species for the gardener to consider; although there are more than 40 biennials in this genus, it would be a brave gardener who would want to grow all of these thistles. The two species that are generally grown look basically the same. They are very tall and are branched, giving them the appearance of a giant candelebra. The stems have wavy wings which have a prickle on the crest of every wave. The leaves also have spines. Both the stems and the foliage are covered with grey hairs which gives the whole plant a silvery look, especially when it catches the sunlight. On the top of each stem is a large thistle-like flower, which is just like the classic Scottish symbol: there is a purple tuft of the flower emerging from a rounded base which is covered in silvery hair and spines. H 3m (10ft) or more, S 1.5m (5ft).

Onopordum acanthium

How to obtain You occasionally see Scotch thistles being sold as plants but they dislike being kept in small pots for too long, so it is better to grow your own from seed. This is readily available.

Cultivation Scotch thistles will grow in any reasonable garden soil, but the richer it is, the larger and more impressive the plants will be. Z6.

Propagation Sow the seed in summer in a pot that can be placed in an open frame without heat. Alternatively, if the ground is available, sow where the plants are to flower in the following year. They will self-sow to provide plants for subsequent years.

Uses These plants are best used at the back of mixed borders. They could be used in bedding schemes; however, they would have to be planted on a grand scale for this to work.

Onopordum acanthium

This is one of the two main plants that are regularly grown. It is the taller of the two and the most widely available. It conforms to the description above. There are no cultivars.

Onopordum nervosum

This plant is possibly better known under its former name of *O. arabicum* and is still sometimes seen advertised as such. It is slightly smaller than the above, otherwise there is very little difference, in gardening terms, between them. Again, there are no cultivars available.

Papaver nudicaule

Papaver rhoeas 'American Legend'

Papaver somniferum, double form

PAPAVER
Poppy

Poppies make up a large genus of some 70 species of which there are a number of annuals as well as perennials that are grown in the garden. The flowers are cup-shaped and have that crumpled tissue-paper appearance typical of poppies. The main colour is red but there are also white, yellow, orange, lilac and purple. Each flower only lasts a day but there is a succession of buds. Many plants will self-sow and will return the following year if allowed to spread their seed.

How to obtain Annual poppies are best acquired as seed, which is widely available.

Cultivation Any reasonable garden soil in a sunny position will suffice. Z2–3 or 6–7.

Propagation The majority of these plants can be sown where the plants are to flower.

Uses Poppies are good for bedding and for mixed borders. They are excellent for wild-flower gardens and borders.

Papaver commutatum

This plant is an excellent poppy with bright red flowers and a black spot at the base of each petal. Because of this colouring, it is often referred to as the ladybird poppy. H 45cm (18in), S 15cm (6in).

Papaver nudicaule

This is the Iceland poppy, which is also sometimes referred to as *P. croceum*. The flowers come in yellows, oranges, pinks and white. H 30cm (12in) S 15cm (6in).

There are a number of cultivars such as 'Garden Gnome' which is a dwarf form.

Papaver rhoeas

This is the field poppy. In its pure form, it produces bright red flowers. However, there are a number of cultivars, such as 'Fairy Wings' and the Shirley poppies, which carry flowers in a range of soft pastels, including pink and lavender-blue, as well as red. The flowers of the form 'American Legend' are red. H 1m (3ft) S 30cm (12in).

Papaver somniferum

This is the opium poppy. It is a tall plant whose flowers come in a wide range of colours and types: single, semi-double and double. The flowers are mainly shades of red, purple, pink, lavender and white. This species has given rise to a great number of named cultivars including 'Black Peony' which has dark flowers. H 1.5m (5ft) S 45cm (18in).

PELARGONIUM
Pelargonium

This is a very large genus, with some 230 species and thousands of cultivars. After 100 years of being called pelargoniums these plants are still often referred to as geraniums. However, they should not be confused with that genus (see pages 53). They are mainly perennials but are usually treated as annuals in the garden. They are used both as foliage and flowering plants. The flowers tend to be carried in tight clusters, which are held on upright or trailing stems. There is a wide range of flower colour, based on shades of red, pink, orange, purple and white. The leaves are valued for their patterning or scent.

There are four basic groups of pelargonium. These are: ivy-leaved, which tend to be trailing and so are good for hanging baskets and window boxes; zonal, which have patterned leaves that are usually green and brown but also come in yellow and red; regal, with larger almost azalea-shaped flowers; and the scented-leaved varieties, which tend to have looser heads of less showy flowers. Heights and spreads are highly variable.

Papaver nudicaule 'Garden Gnome'

Papaver somniferum

Pelargonium 'Ashley Stephenson'

Pelargonium 'Shone Helena'

Pelargonium 'Little Gem'

Perilla frutescens var. crispa

How to obtain Pelargoniums are widely available from many outlets. For a better selection get the catalogues of the specialist nurseries. Some varieties are available as seed.

Cultivation In containers use a good quality potting compost (soil mix). In the open garden plant in reasonably fertile soil which is free-draining. These plants need a position in sun or partial shade. Z8.

Propagation Take cuttings of plants throughout the growing season. Sow seed in early spring under glass at 13–18°C (55–64°F).

Uses Pelargoniums can be used in containers of all sorts or as bedding plants. They can also be planted in general beds.

Ivy-leaved varieties

Cultivars include 'Alice Crousse', whose flowers are cerise-pink, 'Lachsköningin' (semi-double salmon-pink), 'Mme Crousse' (soft pink), and 'Wood's Surprise' (pink and white).

Zonal varieties

'Belinda Adams' has double flowers which are white, flushed with pink, 'Bird Dancer' comes in pink shades, and Century Series (seed-raised) produces red, pink or white flowers. Other good cultivars include 'Francis Parrett', which has double, purple-pink flowers, 'Irene' (semi-double, cerise blooms), 'Mme Fournier' (scarlet flowers, purple foliage) and Video Series (seed-raised, red and pink blooms).

Regal varieties

Good regal varieties include 'Ann Hoystead', which has deep red and black flowers and 'Bredon', also red and black. Other cultivars include 'Carisbrooke' (pink and red), 'Lord Bute' (red and black), and 'Sefton' (cerise and red).

Scented-leaved varieties

Recommended plants in this category include 'Attar of Roses' (mauve flowers), 'Copthorne' (mauve and purple), *P. crispum* 'Variegatum' (lemon-scented variegated leaves and mauve flowers), 'Mabel Grey' (purple), *P. tomentosum* (white flowers and peppermint-scented).

PERILLA
Perilla

A small genus of six plants, of which one, *P. frutescens*, has become very popular in recent years. This is not for its flowers but more for its foliage. The large oval leaves are green but heavily marked with purple and the margins are highly toothed. They are also fragrant. The small flowers are carried in spikes above and among the foliage. They are white or very pale pink. H 1m (3ft) S 30cm (12in) in good conditions, but is often less.

How to obtain Perillas are obtainable as plants from garden centres and nurseries. They are also available as seed.

Cultivation Plant out in a rich soil that is moisture retentive. Perillas can be grown in either sun or light shade. Z8.

Propagation Sow the seed in early spring under glass at 13–18°C (55–64°F).

Uses These plants are good in all forms of foliage schemes. They are very good plants for bedding, especially in exotic schemes. They can also be useful for large containers such as tubs.

Perilla frutescens

This is the plant described above. Its variety *crispa* is even better. It has deep purple leaves that are very frilled around the edge, making it an exotic-looking plant. 'Checkerboard Mixed' is a new cultivar which is a mixture of green and purple plants.

Pelargonium 'Fragaris'

Annual grasses

Agrostis nebulosa	*Lagurus ovatus*
Aira	*Lamarckia aurea*
Avena sterilis	*Panicum capillare*
Briza maxima	*Panicum miliaceum*
Briza minor	*Pennisetum setaceum*
Bromus briziformis	*Pennisetum villosum*
Chloris barbata	*Setaria glauca*
Chloris truncata	*Setaria italica*
Chloris virgita	*Sorghum nigrum*
Hordeum jubatum	*Zea mays*

Petunia 'Blue Daddy'

Petunia 'Blue Wave'

PETUNIA
Petunia

This large genus of 40 species has produced some excellent garden plants. They were originally developed as bedding plants. As containers became more popular, they were bred for that purpose as well, resulting in the magnificent plants that we see today in hanging baskets. The petunia is probably now the favourite plant for baskets, especially since new cultivars produce flowers that have not only had their colour enhanced but which have been made more weather-proof as well. The slightly hairy stems are covered for very long periods with trumpet-shaped flowers. They come in a wide range of colours, mainly based on shades of red, pink and purple, but including white and yellow. Many of them

have a contrasting coloured eye and often darker veining. H up to 45cm (18in) but usually less. The spread varies but trailing forms can grow 1m (3ft) across.
How to obtain Petunias are very widely available as plants in bedding packs or in individual pots from a large range of outlets. Seed is also easy to come by, although there is a bigger range in plant form.
Cultivation Any good potting compost (soil mix) will do for containers and a well-drained soil should be chosen for open-ground planting. Plant in full sun. Z7.
Propagation Sow the seed in the autumn under glass at 16–18°C (60–64°F).
Uses Petunias have many garden uses, but they are particularly good for hanging baskets and other containers.

Petunia Daddy Series
This is a good series, which produces flowers of mixed colours. Some are available as single colours. These include 'Sugar Daddy' which has pink flowers with purple veins, and 'Blue Daddy', which has bluish-purple flowers with darker veins.

Petunia Mirage Series
Another excellent series which has good weather-tolerance. Individual colours are available.

Petunia Picotee Series
The flowers of this series come in pure colours, such as blue or pink, but have a white margin.

Petunia Storm Series
This series includes plants with individual colours such as 'Storm Lavender' and 'Storm Pink'.

Petunia Surfinia Series
A magnificent modern series that has transformed hanging baskets. The purple form 'Surfinia Purple' is particularly good.

Petunia Wave Series
This series includes individual colours, such as 'Blue Wave' and 'Purple Wave'.

Petunia Ultra Star Series
Plants in this series have striped petals, giving them a star-like appearance. The colours are bright blues and reds.

PHACELIA
Scorpion weed

This is a large genus containing 150 species, of which several annuals are widely grown in our gardens. This is partly because they are attractive and partly because they are very good plants for attracting bees, hoverflies and other beneficial insects. Phacelia is now sometimes planted beside agricultural crops for this very reason. The flowers are generally blue and have protruding stamens which sometimes gives them a delightful fuzzy look. The flowers are cup-shaped and are born in clusters over a long period. The plants in this genus vary considerably in height.
How to obtain Phacelias may occasionally be found as plants but it is more common to grow them from seed.
Cultivation Any reasonable garden soil will suffice. Choose a sunny location. Z8.

Petunia 'Storm Lavender'

Phacelia campanularia

Phacelia tanacetifolia

Phaseolus 'Painted Lady' (with creeper)

Propagation Sow the seed in spring in open ground where the plants are to grow.

Uses Phacelias make excellent bedding material and can also be used to good effect in mixed borders. They are a useful addition to wildlife gardens.

Phacelia campanularia

This plant is sometimes known as the Californian bluebell. It has dark blue, upward-facing flowers. There is also a white form. H 30cm (12in).

Phacelia tanacetifolia

The best species for insects, with finely cut leaves and blue blooms. A tall plant, it may need support in exposed positions. H up to 1.2m (4ft) S 45cm (18in).

Other plants *Phacelia viscida* is a medium-sized plant, usually up to 30cm (12in) tall. It has very dark blue flowers with a white eye. There is also a cultivar, called 'Tropical Surf', but it is the same as the species.

PHASEOLUS
Runner bean

The runner bean plant, also known as the climbing bean, can be a very attractive choice for a border. As climbers, these plants are valuable in that they can bring height to a mixed border or bedding scheme. They can be grown up a wigwam of poles or a framework; the dense foliage soon covers the support. The flowers are mainly scarlet but there are also forms that produce pink, white and purple flowers. The pods of some varieties are also very decorative. All in all, an extremely valuable plant, especially since you can eat the beans. H 3m (10ft) S 30cm (12in).

How to obtain These plants are often sold in packs or pots at garden centres. You cannot be sure what colour the flowers will be, but they are usually red. If you want to be certain, grow beans from seed; seed merchants offer hundreds of cultivars.

Cultivation Plant out after the threat of frost has passed in a soil enriched with plenty of well-rotted organic material. It should be moisture retentive. A sunny position is required. Some form of support will be needed. Z8.

Propagation Sow seeds under glass in individual pots in mid-spring or set the seed where the plants are to flower in late spring.

Uses These plants can be used as climbers up poles in a border or over a pergola. They can also be grown in containers, perhaps creating a backdrop for other plants. They can also be used as centrepieces in potagers.

Runner beans in general

These plants have scarlet flowers. They are attractive in their own right but there are plenty of alternatives, and some cultivars carry flowers of several colours, or bicoloured blooms. 'White Lady', as the name suggests, has white flowers, while 'Painted Lady' has red and white blooms and 'Sunset' has soft pink ones. 'Summer Medley' is quite spectacular, producing an array of red, white and pink flowers. 'Relay' carries flowers of several colours. For those that like variegated foliage 'Sun Bright' has green leaves that are flushed with gold.

PHLOX
Phlox

This is a large genus of 67 species of which a number of perennials are in cultivation as well as one popular annual. This is *P. drummondii*. It has long been popular as a bedding plant and seems to have lost none of its appeal, mainly because it has adapted well to life in containers. It is a bushy plant with flowers that are similar in shape to those of the perennial: flat discs on a narrow tubular base. They come in a wonderful range of colours from soft pastels to colours that hit you between the eyes. H up to 45cm (18in) but often much less, S 25cm (10in).

How to obtain These are frequently seen as plants in garden centres, but there is much more choice to be had by purchasing seed.

Cultivation The annual phlox will grow in any reasonable garden soil. Use a good-quality general potting compost (soil mix) in containers. It will grow in either part shade or full sun so long as the soil is moist enough. Z4.

Propagation Sow the seed under glass in early spring at 13–16°C (55–60°F).

Uses The traditional use for this plant is in bedding schemes, but it works equally well in mixed borders or in containers. Taller varieties are good for cutting.

Phlox drummondii

This plant is rarely sold as a species; it is more commonly seen as one of its cultivars of which there are quite a number. 'Tapestry Mixture' and 'Ethnie Pastel Shades' produce a range of soft colours while 'African Sunset' is brilliant red. 'Sternenzauber' or 'Twinkle' has unique star-like flowers with irregularly pointed petals. 'Petticoat' is a dwarf mixture with small flowers. 'Red Admiral' has luscious dark crimson flowers, while 'Grammy Pink White' has striking pink and white flowers.

Phlox drummondii 'Grammy Pink White'

Plectranthus argentatus

PLECTRANTHUS
Plectranthus

This is an enormous genus of more than 370 species. However, from the annual gardener's point of view there is only one of interest. This is *P. forsteri*, which is sometimes called *P. coleoides* and often sold as such. In fact it is a perennial, but it is treated as an annual by most gardeners. The attraction of this plant is not its flowers but its foliage. The leaves are oval and toothed, rather in the manner of nettles. They grow on trailing stems which makes this plant ideal for use in containers of all types, but especially hanging baskets. The small flowers are carried in whorls at the ends of the stems. They are tubular and resemble those of the deadnettles or thyme plants. Their colour is white or mauve. H 25cm (10in) high, S 1m (3ft).

How to obtain Plectranthus is usually purchased as a plant from garden centres. It is sometimes available from florists.

Cultivation Use a good-quality general potting compost (soil mix) if, as is very likely, you are growing these plants in some kind of container. If used in the open garden, any reasonable garden soil will suffice, as long as it is free-draining. Z10.

Propagation Take stem cuttings at any time of year and overwinter the resulting plants.

Uses The primary use for this plant is in containers. It works well in all types of container, but especially in those where the stems can hang down, such as hanging baskets or tall pots. It can also be used as bedding and as a house plant.

Plectranthus forsteri

This plant, which is described above, has light green leaves. However, there is a cultivar which is much more commonly seen. This is *P.f.* 'Marginatus', which has attractive creamy-white margins around the leaf.

Other plants Plectranthus argentatus has become increasingly popular as a bedding plant. The foliage is furry and grey in colour. From this spikes of small, pale pink or bluish flowers arise. It can grow to 1m (3ft) but when used as annual bedding it reaches less than half of this height.

PORTULACA
Sun plant

This is a large genera, this time containing about 100 species. Of these there is only one annual in general cultivation. This is the sun plant, *P. grandiflora*, which is sometimes also called the rose moss. It is a native of sandy places in South America and is a perfect plant for either bedding or containers. It has bluish-green, succulent leaves and flowers that in some ways resemble poppies with their tissue-paper petals and shallow cup shape. The flowers come in a wide range of bright colours, including oranges, reds and pinks, as well as white. H and S 20cm (8in).

How to obtain Sun plants are occasionally available as plants from garden centres but the main source is seed from the various seed merchants.

Cultivation Sun plants need a light, dry soil and a warm sunny position. If growing in a container use a free-draining compost (soil mix). Z10.

Propagation Sow the seed under glass in early spring at 13–18°C (55–60°F).

Uses These are good plants for bedding schemes if the soil is right. They are also ideal for gravel gardens. Their trailing habit makes them suitable for containers, especially hanging baskets and window boxes.

Portulaca grandiflora

Sun plants are sold as mixtures or as individual cultivars. Some mixtures can also be obtained as individual colours. The Sundial hybrids, for example, come as 'Sundial Mango' and 'Sundial Peppermint' as well as in mixed colours. Other mixtures include the Sundance hybrids and Minilace hybrids. One of the most beautiful cultivars is the pure white 'Sun State White'.

Other plants Portulaca oleracea is becoming increasingly available. It is a trailing plant with yellow, orange or pink flowers.

Portulaca grandiflora 'Sundial Mixed'

Reseda odorata

RESEDA
Mignonette

This is another large genus, this time containing about 60 species. One species in the genus is widely grown. This is *R. odorata*, which has been a popular plant in cottage-style gardens for centuries. It has an untidy habit, which fits in well with this type of informal gardening, but it is also very fragrant, a characteristic of so many old-fashioned flowers. The perfume is its main attraction since, while the flowers are pleasant, they are not overly decorative, or at least not when judged alongside more showy flowering plants such as the pelargonium or petunia. The blooms are very small and whitish-yellow with noticeable red anthers. They are carried in spikes which rise up from the sprawling plants. H 45cm (18in) S 30cm (12in).

How to obtain Occasionally mignonettes are seen for sale as plants, but the surest way to obtain them is to grow them from seed, available from some seed merchants and also from specialist society seed lists.

Cultivation Any reasonable garden soil will do for these plants, but it should be well-drained. A sunny position is preferred, especially if you want the scent. Z8.

Propagation Sow the seed in spring in open ground where the plants are to grow.

Uses Excellent for informal displays, including cottage-style gardens. Mignonettes can also be used in imaginative bedding schemes. It is wonderful for wild-flower gardens and borders, and is attractive to bees.

Reseda odorata

This, the main species, is usually grown in its own right. However, there are cultivars available. These do not vary greatly from the species, but 'Red Monarch' has more pronounced red anthers. The flowers of 'Grandiflora' are more yellow, while those of 'Alba' are whiter.

Other plants There are one or two other species that are also available if you hunt hard enough. *R. alba*, which produces creamy white flowers is one, and the much taller *R. luteola*, which carries yellow flowers, is another.

RICINUS
Castor oil plant

This is a single species genus. The species is *R. communis*, which has been part of the bedding scene since Victorian times and probably before that. Although attractive, it is poisonous if eaten. The seed is particularly toxic – the deadly poison ricin is made from it. If there is any doubt as to safety – for example if children visit your garden – do not grow it. Its attraction is its foliage, although if the summer is long and hot enough it will flower. It has large palmate (like fingers radiating from a hand) leaves. In

Ricinus communis

the species these are green but there are also some excellent purple-leaved forms available. When flowers are formed, they are red or pink fuzzy balls and are carried in a spike. In the wild, this plant grows to 12m (40ft) but in the garden it is more like 1.2m (4ft) or less. S 60cm (24in).

How to obtain You can buy these as plants but do not rely on being able to find them. It is better to grow them from seed which is commonly available.

Cultivation Plant out after the threat of frosts has passed in a well-drained but rich soil. This plant requires a warm sunny position. Z10.

Propagation Sow the seed in spring: soak it in water for 24 hours first and then sow under glass at 21°C (70°F).

Uses Castor oil plants can be used as centrepieces in bedding schemes or can be added to a mixed border. They look particularly good in exotic arrangements. These plants can also be grown in large tubs or containers (they do not do well in small pots).

Ricinus communis

This is the only species and it is widely grown. However, the red or bronze-leaved forms are more commonly seen. 'Carmencita' is one of the best; it produces good red foliage and red flowers. 'Carmencita Pink' is similar but produces pink flowers. 'Gibsonii' has dark green foliage with red veins and pinkish flowers. 'Zanzibariensis' is similar but the foliage has white veins.

RUDBECKIA
Coneflower

This is a genus of about 20 species. Most of those used in the garden are perennials. However, there is one biennial and a handful of hybrids that are very much in use. They are popular both because of their vibrant colour and because they tend to flower over a long period, including the autumn. They have daisy-like flowers which have a ring of yellow or gold outer petals. These surround a brown inner disc which is raised in a rounded cone,

Rudbeckia 'Prairie Sun'

hence the name coneflower. They can reach up to 2m (6ft) but rarely do in cultivation. Usual height 60–100cm (2–3ft) S 45cm (18in).

How to obtain Coneflowers are available both as plants and seed from garden centres.

Cultivation Coneflowers will grow in any reasonable garden soil, so long as it does not dry out too much. Conversely, the soil must also be free-draining so there is no waterlogging. Z4.

Propagation Sow the seed in the early spring under glass at 16–18°C (60–64°F).

Uses These plants can be used to good effect in either bedding or mixed borders. They are especially useful in borders that are made up of hot colours.

Rudbeckia hirta

This is the main biennial (treated as an annual) that is cultivated. It is grown as the species and there are also a number of cultivars. 'Bambi' is a short form 30cm (12in) high with attractive gold and bronze petals. 'Gloriosa' has large heads 15cm (6in) wide with golden flowers and sometimes bicolours. It has a double equivalent, 'Double Gloriosa'. 'Irish Eyes' (or 'Green Eyes') has yellow outer petals with an olive green inner ring. 'Kelvedon Star' is an old favourite with yellow flowers flushed with mahogany. 'Toto' has golden-yellow flowers with a brown centre. There are also a number of hybrids available, some of which are listed below.

Rudbeckia 'Goldilocks'

A popular long-flowering plant with semi-double or double golden-yellow flowers.

Rudbeckia 'Marmalade'

Another favourite, this time with large flowers which are yellow ageing to a rich gold.

Rudbeckia 'Prairie Sun'

This attractive plant produces golden-yellow flowers with pale green centres.

Rudbeckia 'Rustic Dwarfs'

These plants have flowers of mixed colours: yellow, gold, mahogany and bronze.

Rudbeckia hirta 'Toto'

Salpiglossis 'Splash Mixed'

Salpiglossis sinuata 'Bolero Mixed'

SALPIGLOSSIS
Salpiglossis

A small genus of two species. One of them, *S. sinuata*, is grown in gardens. There was a time when this plant was very popular but, although it is still grown, it is not seen as frequently as it once was. This is a shame since it is a very attractive plant with large trumpet-shaped flowers, rather like those of petunias. The flowers are carried in great profusion, sometimes smothering the plant. The colours include shades of red, orange, yellow and purple. The veins in the petals are either a darker version of the same colour or a contrasting colour; most of them are bicolours. The height varies between 30 and 60cm (12–24in) S 30cm (12in).

How to obtain Salpiglossis can sometimes be found as plants in garden centres, but this cannot be relied upon. If you are determined to grow them it is safer to grow your own from seed which is readily available from a number of seed merchants.
Cultivation Plant out after the threat of frost has passed. These plants do best in a fertile soil that does not dry out too much. They should have a warm, sunny position. Z8.
Propagation Sow the seed in early spring under glass at 18–21°C (64–70°F).
Uses Salpiglossis make excellent bedding plants, but they can be used to fill gaps in a mixed border. They are also suitable for large containers.

Salpiglossis sinuata
Although the species is sometimes grown in its own right, its cultivars are much more common. Many of these are sold as mixes, such as 'Casino Mixed', 'Splash Mixed' or 'Bolero Mixed'. In others, such as 'Ingrid', 'Kew Blue' and 'Ice Maiden', the colours tend to be similar in each plant although there is still a little variation, usually in the markings.

SALVIA
Sage

This is an enormous genus of 900 species that includes shrubs, perennials and annuals. Of the last there is only one that is grown to any extent. This is *Salvia viridis* which until recently was known as *S. hormium* and is still often listed as such in seed catalogues. This is a true annual, and there are also several short-lived perennials that are used as annuals. One such, *S. splendens* is the perfect bedding plant and is nearly always grown as an annual.
How to obtain Salvia splendens and *S. viridis* are offered in bedding packs and individual pots, as well as being widely available as seed from merchants and others. The other short-lived perennials are occasionally available as plants but can be more reliably found as seed. Seed also gives a greater choice of cultivars.
Cultivation Most will grow in any reasonable garden soil so long as it is free-draining. A warm, sunny position is to be preferred. Z9.
Propagation Sow seed of *S. viridis* in spring in the open ground where they are to flower. Sow seed of other species under glass at 13–16°C (55–60°F).
Uses Both types can be used as summer bedding. The tender perennials are often used in mixed borders or in containers.

Salvia splendens
This short-lived perennial was once the king of bedding plants. It is still used but it is nowhere

Salpiglossis sinuata 'Ice Maiden'

Salvia viridis 'White Swan'

Salvia viridis 'Pink Sundae'

Self-sowing annuals

Atriplex hortensis 'Rubra'	*Limnanthes douglasii*
Borago officinalis	*Lunaria annua*
Calendula officinalis	*Myosotis*
Chrysanthemum segetum	*Nigella*
Collomia grandiflora	*Oenothera biennis*
Digitalis purpurea	*Omphalodes linifolia*
Eryngium giganteum	*Onopordum*
Euphorbia lathyris	*Papaver*
Galactites tomentosa	*Silybum marianum*
Hesperis matronalis	*Verbascum*

near as popular as it once was. It is a bushy plant with spikes of very bright scarlet flowers. H 40cm (16in) S 30cm (12in). There are still a large number of cultivars, some of which now include other colours such as purples and creams. The Sizzler Series is one example.

Salvia viridis

This is the true annual. It is an upright plant which is grown for its spikes of pink, purple or cream bracts. The flowers are insignificant, but the uppermost leaves are coloured in this magnificent way. There are a number of cultivars to choose from including 'White Swan', which has creamy-white bracts with green veins. 'Pink Sundae' produces carmine-coloured bracts. H 45cm (18in) S 25cm (10in).

Other plants The other short-lived perennials include species such as *Salvia coccinea* and its cultivars with scarlet flowers, *S. farinacea* with deep blue flowers, and *S. argentea* with beautiful large, silver leaves.

SANVITALIA
Creeping zinnia

This is a small genus containing a mere seven species of which *S. procumbens* is the only species seen in cultivation. This is a low, creeping plant as its common name implies. Also as the name indicates, the flowers are similar to those of the zinnia, to which it is related. They are daisy-like with an outer ring of bright yellow petals and a large inner disc which is purple-brown. The flowers are not very large, measuring only 2cm (¼in) across, but what they lack in size is more than

Sanvitalia procumbens 'Profusion Cherry'

Sanvitalia procumbens

compensated for by the quantity produced. H 20cm (8in) S 45cm (18in).

How to obtain Sanvitalias can be purchased as bedding or container plants from garden centres and nurseries. They are also available as seed from merchants, which provide a large choice of cultivars.

Cultivation Plant in any reasonable garden soil. A sunny position is to be preferred. Z8.

Propagation Sow the seed where the plants are to flower in autumn or spring. Sow under glass at 13–16°C (55–60°F) in early spring for container plants.

Uses These make excellent bedding plants. They are also suitable for containers.

Sanvitalia procumbens

This is the only species generally cultivated, and is described above. There are also a number of cultivars. These include 'Irish Eyes' whose flowers have green centres and 'Mandarin Orange' which has bright orange petals and a brown centre. 'Dwarf Carpet' reaches only 10cm (4in) in height. 'Profusion Cherry' is a lovely shade of red, and 'Sprite' is a yellow and brown semi-double.

Scabiosa atropurpurea 'Chile Pepper'

SCABIOSA
Scabious

This is a large genus containing about 80 species of perennials and a few annuals. Both the annuals and the perennials have a similar type of flower, which is probably best described as a pincushion. It consists of a dome of florets, with the outer ones often being larger than the inner ones. Generally the flower colour is lavender-blue but in the annuals there is some variation. The flowers are carried on slender stems above finely cut foliage, making these very attractive, delicate-looking plants. There is a certain old-fashioned quality about them that makes the scabious an ideal addition to informal schemes, such as that of a cottage garden.

Scabiosa stellata

How to obtain They are available as plants in individual pots from garden centres and nurseries. Seed is also widely available.
Cultivation Any reasonable garden soil will be sufficient so long as it is not waterlogged. Scabious make good cut flowers and some of the seed head can be dried. Z6.
Propagation Sow the seed in mid-spring in the open ground where it is to flower. Alternatively sow in pots under glass at 13–16°C (55–60°F).
Uses Scabious are probably best used in mixed borders although they can also be used as bedding.

Scabiosa atropurpurea
This is a superb plant with pincushion flower heads that vary from lavender to deep purple. It grows to 1m (3ft) when growing well but is often less. S 30cm (12in). There are several cultivars of which 'Chile Pepper' is the current favourite. This has very dark red flowers with speckles of white. 'Blue Cockade' has large heads twice the size of most (up to 5cm/2in across) with lavender to purple flowers.

Scabiosa stellata
This plant has pale blue pincushions. When the flower fades, these turn into spherical seed heads with each seed being framed in a ruff. They make excellent dried flowers.

Other plants Scabiosa prolifera has cream-coloured flower heads and, like the previous plant, produces papery seed heads that are good for drying. It is more difficult to find than the other species.

SCAEVOLA
Fairy fan flower

The scaevola is a large genus of about 90 species of which only one is in general cultivation. This is *S. aemula*, the fairy fan flower or the cushion fan flower. It is a curious plant that is perfect for hanging baskets but is not quite so useful in the borders. It is a low-growing, spreading plant. The flowers are lavender blue and the five petals are in the shape of a fan. H 15cm (6in) S 1m (3ft).

Scaevola aemula 'Blue Wonder'

How to obtain Scaevolas are generally sold as small plants by a few garden centres and by mail order. Seed can be obtained but this is not so satisfactory as named plants.
Cultivation Plant out in a moist, reasonably rich soil that is free-draining. In containers use a good general potting compost (soil mix). Scaevola can be planted in full sun, so long as the soil is kept moist, or in light shade. Z10.
Propagation Take cuttings in summer and overwinter the young plants under glass. Seed can be sown under glass at 18–21°C (64–70°F).
Uses Its spreading habit makes the scaevola ideal as a container plant, especially in hanging baskets. It can also be used as an unusual bedding plant.

Scaevola aemula 'Blue Wonder' (detail)

Scaevola aemula
The species can be grown from seed but the plants are not particularly floriferous. The forms 'Blue Wonder' and 'Blue Fan' produce a lot more flowers and are worth obtaining. They both have lilac-blue flowers. There is also a form called 'Mauve Clusters' in which the flowers are slightly more mauve. However, there is not a great deal to choose between the cultivars. In the wild the flowers can be white; hard searching might locate the seed of such plants.

SCHIZANTHUS
Butterfly flower

This is a genus of about 15 species of annuals and biennials. Several are in cultivation, but only one, *S. pinnatus*, and its cultivars and hybrids are used to any great extent. They are not quite so popular as they once were but they are still well worth growing since they are spectacular plants. In well-grown specimens it is impossible to see the plant for the flowers. The English name is very apt – the flowers are like butterflies. The alternative name of poor man's orchids is also true since they are very exotic looking. They are very colourful: the basic flower colouring is shades of pink with a yellow and white centre with orange spotting. H 45cm (18in) S 30cm (12in).
How to obtain Schizanthus can be bought as plants in individual pots but if you can raise them it

Schizanthus pinnatus cultivars

Silene coeli-rosa 'Royal Celebration'

is better to buy seed since you will get a better choice and many more plants.

Cultivation For container plants choose a good-quality general potting compost (soil mix). In the open ground, any well-drained soil that does not dry out excessively will do. Plant in a warm sunny position. Pinch the growing tips out to make the plants bushy. Z10.

Propagation Sow seed in early spring under glass at 16–18°C (60–64°F).

Uses Schizanthus are magnificent plants for containers. They also look superb as massed bedding.

Schizanthus pinnatus

This is the main species grown, and is described above. It has several cultivars and is also one

Schizanthus pinnatus

of the parents of the next plant listed. Cultivars often come in mixed colours. They include 'Angel's Wings', 'Disco Mixed', 'Hit Parade', 'Star Parade', and the rather uninspiringly named 'Giant Hybrids'.

Schizanthus × wisetonensis

This is an excellent hybrid of the above. It also has a number of cultivars, none of which is very different from the others.

SILENE
Campion

This is one of the most important genera in gardening terms since so many of the 500 species are grown in our gardens. They include perennials and annuals. On the whole they are not very showy plants but they do provide a backbone to plantings. There are several annuals which are of interest. The flowers are generally five-petalled discs in various shades of pink or white.
H 15–45cm (6–18in) S up to 25cm (10in).

How to obtain The plants may be seen in garden centres but they are more likely to be found in nurseries. Seed is available from seed merchants, although you may have to check out specialist society seed lists for rarer seed.

Cultivation Silene will grow in any garden soil, in either sun or shade. Z7.

Propagation Most annuals can be sown in the the spring in the open ground where the plants are

to flower. They can also be sown in pots under glass at 13–16°C (55–60°F).

Uses These plants can be used in a wide variety of garden sites. They fit well into a mixed border and some can be used in bedding or containers.

Silene coeli-rosa

This plant is commonly known as the rose of heaven and was once very popular. It looks rather like a large-flowered gypsophila. The notched petals are pink, fading to white at the base. There are several good cultivars available. The Angel Series includes 'Rose Angel' which produces rose-pink flowers and 'Blue Angel' which has lavender-blue flowers. 'Royal Celebration' carries blooms in a good mixture of colours.

Silene pendula

This attractive plant has been reintroduced in recent years in the form 'Peach Blossom'. This is a little gem which grows to no more than 15cm (6in) in height and about the same in spread. The double flowers come in shades of delicate pale pink. There is also a white form, also with double flowers, called 'Snowball', while 'Triumph' produces blooms of deep pink.

Other plants *Silene armeria* is a delightful plant with powdery grey-green leaves and stems and domes of small flowers in a deep rose-pink. It self-sows without becoming a nuisance. There is a free-flowering form called 'Electra' which carries flowers of a darker pink.

Silene pendula 'Peach Blossom'

Silene armeria 'Rose Angel'

Silybum marianum

Smyrnium perfoliatum

SILYBUM
Milk thistle

This is a small genus of two similar plants. The one that is most widely grown in gardens is *S. marianum*, which is known as the milk thistle or St Mary's thistle. It is valued mainly for its foliage. The leaves are large with deep lobes, each topped with a spine. They are a glossy green and covered with a random white marbling, which looks rather like spilt milk or St Mary's milk, hence the plant's name. They are very attractive leaves indeed.

The flowers are just like those of a typical thistle, with purple tufts erupting from a cup of spiny bracts. The thistle will normally spread 1m (3ft) wide when grown in good ground, but if it is in very rich soil it can grow to twice that and become huge. However, 60cm (24in) is the normal expected width and 1m (3ft) the height. If your silybum do grow very large, they can smother the surrounding plants.

How to obtain You will rarely find plants for sale, but silybum is available as seed from a variety of sources. It is usually found in specialist society seed exchanges.

Cultivation Any reasonable garden soil will do for silybum, but the richer the soil, the bigger the plants. Z7.

Propagation Sow the seed in the open ground where the plants are to grow in autumn or spring. It will self-sow if left to seed providing plants for later years.

Uses This is a magnificent foliage plant best suited to the mixed border, or it could be used as bedding in some imaginative scheme. If you are not worried about the sharp spines it can make an interesting addition to children's gardens, not least because most children find the name highly amusing.

Other plants Although it is not seen very often, the other plant in the genus, *S. eburneum*, is sometimes cultivated in gardens.

SMYRNIUM
Smyrnium

This is a genus of about eight biennial plants. Of these, one is grown quite widely in gardens, while another is occasionally seen. The common one is called *S. perfoliatum*. This is not a plant for neat and tidy, formal gardens, but one that crops up in informal gardens, especially those with shady areas, or in wild-flower gardens. It is a delightful plant, looking rather like a spurge (*Euphorbia*), with its tiny yellowish-green flowers. These appear in late spring. The leaves immediately below the flowers are the same colour and it is these that give the plant its characteristic appearance. H 1m (3ft) when given good conditions, S 30cm (12in).

How to obtain Seed is available from a few seed merchants, but you will have to search for it. It is also available from the seed exchanges of specialist societies. Once you have this plant, it will self-sow.

Cultivation Any reasonable garden soil will suffice. Smyrniums will grow in sun, but they are a useful plant for light shade. Z7.

Propagation Sow the seed in the open ground where the plants are to grow. Alternatively, sow in a pot and place in an open frame without heat. Let the plants self sow for future years.

Uses These plants can be used in informal borders, including cottage gardens, but they are best used in wild-flower gardens, or in shady areas where their bright golden colour shines out.

This looks very similar to *S. marianum*. The seed is available, but it is not easy to find.

Sutera cordata 'Snowflake'

Sutera cordata

Other plants *Smyrnium olusatrum* grows naturally around coasts, and it is good for wild-flower gardens in that kind of area. It is much bigger and more solid than the above with heavy domes of yellow flowers and large glossy leaves. It is very much like a yellow-flowered angelica. It self-sows prodigiously so be careful where you site it.

SUTERA
Sutera

This genus contains 130 species. The one that is grown in gardens is *S. cordata*, which is also known as *Bacopa* 'Snowflake'. It is one of those plants that suddenly takes the gardening world by storm. It was hardly known a few years ago and you would not have been able to find it, but now it is in most garden centres. It is a low creeping plant that is covered in a mass of white flowers, each having five rounded petals. It flowers for a long time and its sprawling habit makes it perfect for hanging baskets, for which it is mainly marketed. H 10–15cm (4–6in) S 45cm (18in).

How to obtain Suteras are available only as plants, not as seed. The cultivar *S. cordata* 'Snowflake' is readily available, but the others listed are not so frequently seen. However, they are gradually becoming more commonplace.

Cultivation Do not plant out suteras until after the threat of frost has passed. Use a good-quality general potting compost (soil mix). Pinch out the side shoots to start with so that your plant becomes bushy. Keep the compost moist; the flowers will drop if it dries out. Z10.

Propagation Take cuttings in summer and overwinter the plants under warm glass.

Uses This is an excellent hanging basket plant, which is one of the reasons it has become so popular. It can also be used in other types of containers. There is also no reason why it should not be planted in walls and such like.

Sutera cordata

The species as such is not usually grown; it is more commonly seen in the form of one of its cultivars. The most popular of these is 'Snowflake' which has small, pure white flowers with a yellow eye. There are several new white forms on offer including 'Snowstorm' and 'Bridal Showers'. There are also a couple of lavender-coloured forms: 'Lavender Storm' and the darker-flowered 'Blue Showers'. There is a pink form, which has no specific name, and a form with golden variegated foliage and white flowers, which is known as 'Olympic Gold'.

Other plants *Sutera grandiflora* has been around for a bit longer. It is a similar spreading plant to the above, but it produces lavender-blue flowers which have a white throat. There are several cultivars.

SYMPHYANDRA
Symphyandra

This is a genus of some 12 short-lived perennials that are usually treated as annuals. They are closely related to the bellflowers, *Campanula*. Quite a few of them are in cultivation but tend to be grown by gardeners who specialize in such plants, such as alpine growers, rather than the general gardener.

There is one, however, that is not difficult to grow and is well worth the effort to find. This is *S. hofmannii*. It grows up to 60cm (24in) high and 30cm (12in) across and is covered with hanging bellflowers of creamy-white. They are each over 2.5cm (1in) in diameter. Symphyandras are not in the same league as many bedding plants, but they do remain flowering for quite a long time during the summer, an attribute which earns them their place in the garden.

How to obtain You can occasionally find symphyandras in specialist nurseries, but if you want to be certain of obtaining plants then the safest way is to get seed. This is available from a number of seed merchants as well as from the seed exchange lists of specialist garden societies.

Cultivation Symphyandras will grow in any reasonable garden soil, but they prefer light, free-draining ones. Choose either a sunny or lightly shaded position for these plants. Z4.

Propagation Sow the seed in early spring under glass at 13–16°C (55–60°F).

Uses These plants are best used in a mixed border. They make an excellent addition to a white garden or white border.

Other plants Most of the other symphyandras are available either as plants or as seed from specialist sources. Most are treated as annuals used in the mixed border or rock garden. They all have bell-shaped flowers and include blue as well as white flowers. *S. pendula* is the next most frequently seen after *S. hofmannii*. This also has white flowers. *S. armena* is a good species if you want pale blue flowers.

Annuals for hanging baskets

Begonia	Nolana humifusa
Bidens	Petunia
Brachyscome	Pelargonium
Chrysanthemum	Sanvitalia procumbens
Echium	Senecio cineraria
Felicia amelloides	Sutera cordata
Helichrysum	Tagetes
Laurentia	Tropaeolum
Lobelia	Verbena
Myosotis	Viola

Symphyandra hofmannii

Tagetes 'French Vanilla'

Tagetes patula 'Safari Tangerine'

TAGETES
Marigolds

This genus of daisy-like plants contains about 50 species. The two that are of most interest to gardeners are the French marigold (*T. patula*) and the African marigold (*T. erecta*). There are also some hybrids between the two as well as some derived from the species *T. tenuifolia*. Many marigold cultivars are in series and they are generally sold as mixtures, but some individual forms are sold.

The basic plants are daisy-like with an outer ring of petals and a central disc. However, many are doubles and semi-doubles. The predominant colour is golden-yellow but orange and mahogany-red also feature prominently. These plants have always played an important part in bedding schemes. In recent years their importance has declined, but the marigolds have retained enough popularity to remain widely available. H 15–45cm (6–18in) S 30cm (12in).

How to obtain Marigolds are available as plants, both in bedding packs and individual pots. However, buying plants restricts your choice of cultivars; growing your own plants from seed opens up hundreds of interesting possibilities.

Cultivation Any reasonable quality garden soil will be suitable so long as it is free-draining. A sunny position is best. Deadhead marigolds regularly to obtain continual flowering. Z9.

Propagation Sow the seed in the early spring under glass at 18–21°C (64–70°F). It can be sown where the plants are to flower but this will result in much later-flowering plants.

Uses These are predominantly plants for bedding schemes, but they can be used in mixed border or even in containers. They are good for children's gardens.

Tagetes Disco Series
This is a single French marigold which comes in a complete range of colours.

Tagetes 'French Vanilla'
A delightful double African marigold with large creamy-coloured flowers.

Tagetes Gem Series
This is a *T. tenuifolia* mixture, with single flowers in yellow and orange. The cultivars 'Golden Gem', 'Lemon Gem' and 'Tangerine Gem' are sold as separate colours.

Tagetes Safari Series
This is a series of double French marigolds including gold, yellow, orange and red flowers, some with mahogany markings.

THUNBERGIA
Thunbergia

This is a genus of more than 100 species. The one that is of most interest to gardeners is *T. alata*, commonly known as the black-eyed Susan. It is actually a perennial but treated like an annual. It must be said that it is welcome in the first place because of its attractive flowers, but the fact that it climbs is definitely a bonus since this is an attribute not often found in annuals. The flowers are funnel-shaped. They are orange in colour with a very noticeable black eye – hence the plant's common name. It is actually a twining plant that reaches about 2m (6ft) in height.

How to obtain Black-eyed Susans are sometimes seen for sale in garden centres and nurseries, but the way to be certain of getting plants is to grow your own from seed. This is readily obtainable from seed merchants

Cultivation Black-eyed Susans can be grown in open ground so long as the soil is moisture-retentive but well drained. A good-quality potting compost (soil mix) should be used for containers.

Tagetes 'Golden Gem'

Tagetes erecta 'Golden Jubilee'

Thunbergia alata

Tithonia rotundifolia 'Goldfinger'

This plant needs to be sited in a warm sunny place. If you are able to keep it warm, move it inside for the winter and reuse it the following year. Z10.

Propagation Sow the seed under glass in early spring at 18–21°C (64–70°F).

Uses The black-eyed Susan can be used in any position where a climbing plant is required. It can be grown up a wigwam of branches in a bedding display or it can climb up a similar structure in a container.

Thunbergia alata

This is the climbing plant described above. The flowers are usually orange or deep yellow although they can also be cream. Most have black eyes but some lack these. It is usually grown as the species but it is sometimes offered as a cultivar such as 'Suzie Hybrids' which is not much different from the species.

Other plants Thunbergia gregorii is another climbing perennial that is treated as an annual. This is similar to the above but lacks the dark eye. It is not so commonly available.

TITHONIA
Mexican sunflower

This is a genus of about ten annuals and perennials of which one, T. rotundifolia, is grown in our gardens. This is not seen anywhere as near as often as it should be since it is a superb plant and those who grow it often rank it as one of their favourites. As with so many annuals, this has daisy-like flowers. In this case the outer ring of petals is a wonderful rich orange and the inner disc is yellow. The flowers are quite large, being up to about 7cm (3in) or more across. They appear at the end of upright stems which swell noticeably just below the flower head. The

plants are bushy and well branched. They are big plants and fill a big impressive space in the border. H 2m (6ft) when growing well, S 45cm (18in) or more.

How to obtain Mexican sunflowers are sometimes seen for sale as plants, but they do not like being confined for too long in a small pot. It is better to buy seed, which is readily available, and grow your own.

Cultivation Plant out after the threat of frosts has passed. These plants need a rich, moist, but free-draining soil and a sunny position. They may need support in exposed positions. Z9.

Propagation Sow the seed under glass at 13–18°C (55–64°F). Do not sow too early, late spring is the right time.

Uses Mexican sunflowers can be used as bedding material but they work best in mixed borders. They can be used in drifts, but a well-grown single specimen can be very impressive. They can be grown in containers, but they must be big.

Tithonia rotundifolia

The species, which is described above, is often grown. There are also a few cultivars. 'Goldfinger' is a more compact plant growing only 75cm (30in) high, making it more suited to bedding. 'Early Yellow' is the same height but with yellow flowers, while 'Torch' is double this height and has large reddish-orange flowers. 'Arcadian Blend' is a mixture of yellow, gold and orange. The single-coloured cultivars tend to look better.

TORENIA
Wishbone flower

This is a genus containing about 50 species of which, as so often happens, only one is widely grown in the garden. In this case it is T. fournieri. This is a bushy plant with masses of trumpet-shaped flowers, which can smother the plant to the extent that the leaves can hardly be seen. The flowers have a pale blue upper lip and a velvety, darker blue-purple lower one. They flower over a long period from midsummer well into autumn. H 30cm (12in) S 20cm (8in).

How to obtain Plants are not often seen for sale but seed is offered by a number of seed merchants. Torenias are not as popular as they once were, so you may have to search for them.

Cultivation Plant out in a rich moist soil in a sheltered position that is lightly shaded. Any good-quality potting compost (soil mix) is suitable for plants used in containers. Do not set these outside before the danger of frosts has been lifted. Z9.

Propagation Sow the seed in mid-spring under glass at 16–18°C (60–64°F).

Uses Torenias can be used as bedding plants in a shady position. They are also very suitable for containers.

Torenia fournieri

This is the main species grown. Seed can be obtained as the species or as one of several cultivars which have different coloured flowers. The Clown Series has pink, white and purple flowers in its mixture. Panda Series is similar except that the plants are more compact, reaching only about 20cm (8in) in height. 'Pink Panda' has pink flowers.

Other plants Torenia flava is sometimes seen on offer as seed. This is a spreading plant which is suitable for hanging baskets. It has small flowers which are a velvety-yellow. You may find them sold under the alternative name of 'Suzy Wong'.

Torenia fournieri Clown Series

Annuals for window boxes

Ageratum	Lobelia
Antirrhinum	Myosotis
Begonia	Nicotiana
Bidens	Nolana humifusa
Cerinthe	Petunia
Chrysanthemum	Pelargonium
Erysimum cheiri	Schizanthus
Exacum affine	Tagetes
Felicia amelloides	Verbena
Helichrysum	Viola

Tropaeolum majus

TROPAEOLUM
Nasturtium

There can be few gardeners who are not familiar with the delightful plants of this genus. There are getting on for 90 species in it, many of which are perennials that make excellent garden plants, but there is one annual in particular which is the darling of the annual grower. This is *T. majus* and its cultivars and hybrids. The typical plant has flame-red trumpet-shaped flowers, but there are quite a few variations on this. It is a trailing or climbing plant and can be used to hang from containers or scramble up through low shrubs. It is an excellent plant for covering large areas. H and S 3m (10ft) or more.
How to obtain You can buy plants but it is better to buy seed. This gives you better plants as well as a much larger choice.
Cultivation Any reasonable garden soil will be sufficient, since nasturtiums will grow in quite poor conditions. A position in full sun is best but plants often self-sow if in light shade. Z8.

Propagation Sow the seed in the spring in the open ground where the plants are to flower.
Uses Nasturtiums are versatile plants that can be used as bedding or in a mixed border. They can be allowed to spread across the ground or a support to climb up. Nasturtiums are good for covering large areas of bare earth. They can be grown in containers, but they must be large.

Tropaeolum majus
The species is often grown in its own right, but it also has a large number of cultivars and hybrids. In these the trumpets may be red, orange, yellow or cream, usually with contrasting markings in the throat. In recent times there has also been a tendency for breeders to produce plants with variegated foliage; some have splashes of pale yellow and others have darker gold markings.
   Cultivars worth considering include: the Alaska Series which has creamy-white variegated leaves and a mixture of flower colours; 'Empress of India', a dwarf plant only 30cm (12in) high which has semi-double red flowers; 'Peach Melba' also with semi-double flowers but this time they are a primrose-yellow colour and have orange markings; 'Red Tiger', a semi-double with orange, red-striped flowers; and 'Milkmaid', which has creamy-yellow flowers.

Other plants *Tropaeolum peregrinum* is known as the canary creeper. It is a vigorous climber that grows up

Ursinia anthemoides 'Solar Fire'

to 3m (10ft), and has dainty little yellow flowers which have delicately cut petals. It is an excellent garden plant.

URSINIA
Ursinia

This is a genus containing about 40 species of perennials and a few annuals. Of these *U. anthemoides* is the main one in cultivation, although there are several others that are occasionally available. This is a plant with finely cut leaves topped by large daisy flower heads, up to 5cm (2in) or more across, carried on tall wiry stems. The ring of outer petals are deep gold or light orange with a purple spot at the base, creating an inner ring of colour. The central disc is also gold. The plants flower over a very long period. H 45cm (18in) S 30cm (12in).
How to obtain Ursinias are occasionally seen as plants for sale

in garden centres and nurseries, but they are usually purchased in the form of seed from some, not all, of the seed merchants.
Cultivation Plant out when frosts have passed in a well-drained light soil. Ursinias can also be grown in a good-quality general potting compost (soil mix). Z8.
Propagation Sow the seed under glass in the early spring at 16–18°C (60–64°F).
Uses The brightness of their colour makes ursinias very suitable as bedding plants, but they can also be used in a mixed border, especially one that is devoted to hot colours.

Ursinia anthemoides
This is the brightly coloured, bushy annual described above. Cultivars such as 'Solar Fire' and 'Sunshine Blend' are sometimes seen but they are not very different from the species.

Tropaeolum peregrinum

Ursinia anthemoides 'Sunshine Blend'

Other plants Several other species in this genus are offered from time to time. These are also yellow- or orange-flowered.

VERBASCUM
Mullein

This is an enormous genus of about 360 species. A fair number of these are in cultivation either as perennials or as annuals. Their great attraction is the tall spikes of flowers that they carry. Some of these are discreet and only reach 60cm (24in) or so, but others are a towering 2.5m (8ft) or more. The plants can produce just one spike or several, creating a candelabra effect. On the whole the saucer-shaped flowers are yellow, but there are also white and purple variations available. The centres of the flowers are usually purple.

How to obtain You occasionally see verbascums for sale in garden centres but they dislike being in small pots for long so it is better to grow them from seed. This is widely available.

Cultivation Plant out or sow in any reasonable garden soil so long as it is free draining. In more exposed positions the taller specimens may need support of some kind. Z6.

Propagation Sow the seed in the spring, in the open ground where the plants are to flower, or sow in pots and place in an open frame without heat. Plants will self-sow.

Uses The architectural quality of verbascums makes them ideal for using as focal points, especially in a mixed border. They could also be used in an imaginative bedding scheme.

Verbascum bombyciferum

This is a biennial that overwinters as a rosette and then pushes up flower stems. The flowers are a soft yellow and the leaves are covered with silvery hairs. A magnificent plant. H 2.5m (8ft).

Other plants There are several other species available, although they are not seen as frequently. *V. thapsus*, known as Aaron's rod or great mullein, is another tall plant which will happily self-sow. It has yellow flowers. *V. sinuatum* is much shorter at about 1m (3ft), but it has many branches, each coming from the base. Again it produces yellow flowers and is a very attractive plant. *V. lychnitis*, or the white mullein, has white flowers.

VERBENA
Verbena

This is a large genus of about 250 species of annuals and perennials. Quite a number of the perennials are tender and are treated as annuals. The annuals are generally low-growing and are often sprawling, making them ideal for containers. They are grown principally for their flowers, which are carried in flat or slightly domed heads. Individually the flowers have five petals and are tubular with an open mouth, like a disc. The colours are

Verbena 'Peaches and Cream'

generally shades of pink, red and purple, each with a white eye. There are also white flowers, which have a cream eye.

How to obtain Verbenas are usually bought as plants in individual pots from garden centres and nurseries. Most offer a good selection of varieties. Some are now offered as seed and these produce some interesting results.

Cultivation Plant out in any reasonable garden soil so long as it is free-draining. Use a good quality general potting compost (soil mix) for plants grown in containers. Z9.

Propagation Take cuttings in the summer and overwinter them under warm glass. Sow seed in early spring under glass at 16–18°C (60–64°F).

Uses Verbenas are excellent all-round plants for the garden. They can be used as bedding plants or grown in a mixed border, and they can also be used to great effect in all types of containers including hanging baskets.

Verbena × hybrida

Most cultivars sold in garden centres come under this heading. They are often offered in series which have mixed colours, such as Derby Series, which are 25cm (10in) high and come in pink and red shades. Novalis Series are the same size but with a wider range of colours. Separate colours are available. Sandy Series and Romance Series are similar. Individual colours are also available, as in the delectable 'Peaches and Cream', which has pink and creamy flowers.

Other plants Other plants to explore include the bright red *V. peruvianna* as well as individual cultivars such as the beautiful *V.* 'Silver Anne' and *V.* 'Sissinghurst'.

Verbascum

Verbena 'Aphrodite'

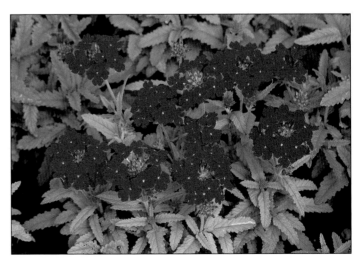
Verbena 'Sandy Scarlet'

Viola tricolor

VIOLA
Viola

This is a vast genus containing 500 species. Many of them are in cultivation as perennials. However, there is one that is widely grown as an annual and that is the pansy *V. × wittrockiana*. This has long been a favourite in gardens, and was once the subject of heated competitions. Pansies tend to be rather sprawling plants with large flowers which often seem to resemble cheeky faces. Nearly all colours are represented, and usually more than one colour is present in each flower. They have long flowering periods, and there are pansies for all times of the year, including winter. Size varies but it is usually in the range of 15–25cm (6–10in) in height and up to 30cm (12in) in spread. Given the opportunity pansies will scramble up the other plants and reach greater heights.

How to obtain Plants are frequently available as bedding packs or individual pots in garden centres and nurseries as well as other outlets such as gas stations. Seed is also widely available and offers a better range.

Propagation Sow seed in early spring under glass at 13–16°C (55–60°F).

Cultivation Any reasonable garden soil will do but it must be moisture-retentive if the plants are set out in full sun. They will also grow in light shade. Trim them back if they get leggy (produce long bare stems). Z6.

Uses Pansies can be used anywhere in the garden, as bedding, in mixed borders or in containers.

Viola × wittrockiana

This is the main annual viola, although it is, in fact, a perennial. There are many cultivars available. Mixtures such as Joker Series also come as individual colours ('Jolly Joker' for example), and there are individual cultivars. These include 'Pretty', with its yellow and mahogany flowers, and 'Scarlet Orange Duet', with its red and orange flowers. The colour range is extensive, but the flowers usually have a yellow eye and frequently have black patches. The best way of looking at these plants is to get the seed merchant's catalogues, which contain hundreds of possibilities.

Other plants The tiny-flowered *Viola tricolor*, commonly known as heartsease, is an annual that is well worth growing. There are several cultivars. They include single-colour flowers, such as 'Bowles' Black' or bicolours. This plant self-sows.

XERANTHEMUM
Xeranthemum

This is a small genus of about six species of annuals, of which one is grown in gardens. These plants were once more widely cultivated, but like so many old-fashioned annuals they are somewhat out of fashion at the moment. This is a pity since they are very attractive, everlasting flowers.

There is quite a wide range of colours, which is based on shades of pink, red and purple. The flowers are daisy-like with an outer ring of coloured petals and a coloured central disc. H 60cm (24in) S 30cm (12in).

How to obtain Xeranthemum are occasionally seen sold as plants but the surest way to obtain them is from seed. This is offered by many seed merchants.

Cultivation Plant Xeranthemum out after the frosts have passed in any reasonable, free-draining garden soil. Give these plants a sunny position. Z9.

Propagation Sow the seed in the spring under glass at 16–18°C (60–64°F).

Uses These can be used as bedding plants or in a mixed border. They make excellent cut flowers and are perfect for drying.

Xeranthemum annuum

This species is still widely grown. It has both single and double flowers, which can be up to 5cm

Xeranthemum annuum 'Superbissima'

(2in) across, but are more often only 2cm (¼in). There are some cultivars: 'Snow Lady', which has white flowers; 'Superbissima' (rich purple); 'Lilac Stars' (lilac); and 'Cherry Ripe' (mixture of bright colours). These plants tend to flower over a very long period from midsummer well into autumn. The silvery-green leaves are covered with fine hairs.

Xeranthemum annuum

Zea mays

ZEA
Maize

This well-known genus has four species. One of them, *Z. mays*, is the much-cultivated maize which is used as a cereal crop throughout the world. Although it is widely grown in the vegetable garden, it is also grown as a decorative plant because it has both interesting foliage and colourful seed heads. The leaves are strap-like and hang down. In some cultivars they are variegated. The seed is carried in large heads, which are commonly known as corn-on-the-cob. The cases split open to display the ranks of individual corn grains. These are normally yellow but can include many other colours, making them look very decorative. The flowers are like silken tassels. These plants are tall and can reach 4m (12ft) but they are generally only half of this.

How to obtain Decorative maize is sometimes seen for sale, although it is best to grow your own plants from the wide variety of seed that is offered.

Cultivation Plant out after the last frosts in a fertile, free-draining soil. These plants require a position in full sun. Z10.

Propagation The seed can be sown, in spring, directly in the soil where the plants are to grow or sown individually in pots under glass at 18°C (64°F).

Uses Decorative maize makes a good foliage or decorative plant for the back of a mixed border. It can be used as temporary hedge.

Zea mays

This is the only species widely grown. It has been described above. It is usually sold as cultivars, either for the vegetable garden or for decorative purposes. 'Harlequin' has striped foliage in green, white and red, and corn in a deep red. Another variegated foliage plant is 'Variegata', whose leaves are striped with white. 'Strawberry Corn' has a mixture of yellow and red corn.

ZINNIA
Zinnia

The annuals of this genus of 20 species are still popular and there are many different varieties available. They are grown for their showy flowers, which are like large daisies with wide petals. They are often semi-doubles or doubles. There is a wide range of colours. Unusually, this includes green, but shades of yellow, orange, red and purple are more common. In good specimens the flowers can be up to 12cm (4½in) across. Their long stems make them suitable for cutting. H 75cm (30in) S 30cm (12in).

How to obtain Zinnias are frequently offered for sale as plants in individual pots at garden centres, nurseries and other outlets. They are also available in a wide range of seed from most seed merchants.

Propagation Sow the seed in mid-spring under glass at 13–18°C (55–64°F).

Cultivation Plant out only after all danger of frosts has passed. Choose a fertile soil to which plenty of well-rotted organic material has been added. Zinnias must have a warm and sunny position. Deadheading helps them to flower over a long period. Z10.

Uses They make excellent bedding plants or can be used in mixed borders. They can also be grown in larger containers, such as tubs.

Zinnia elegans

This is the taller of the two species commonly cultivated and the flowers are usually larger. The species is rarely grown in its own right; it is much more commonly seen as one of its many cultivars. These are generally offered as mixtures. Some, including the Profusion Series are also available as individual colours such as 'Profusion White' and 'Profusion Cherry'. The Dasher Series is similar, with 'Dasher Orange'. There are several dwarf series:

Zinnia elegans 'Profusion Cherry'

Peter Pan Series, Short Stuff Series and Small Wonder Series. Some cultivars are single coloured, such as the pale green 'Envy'.

Zinnia haageana

This is still often referred to by its former name, *Z. angustifolia*. The plants are not as big as the previous ones, but they also have broad petals. These are usually bright orange, but yellow and mahogany-red also feature among the cultivars. 'Orange Star' has pure, deep orange flowers; 'Persian Carpet' has semi-double and double flowers that are yellow or orange, splashed with mahogany.

Zinnia elegans 'Profusion White'

Zinnia elegans 'Dasher Orange'

Index

Begonia semperflorens

Dahlia 'Hamari Katrina'

Plant hardiness zones

Plant entries in this book have been given zone numbers, and these zones relate to their hardiness. The zonal system used, shown below, was developed by the Agricultural Research Service of the U.S. Department of Agriculture. According to this system, there are 11 zones, based on the average annual minimum temperature in a geographical zone.

When a range of zones is given for a plant, the smaller number indicates the northernmost zone in which a plant can survive the winter, and the higher number gives the most southerly area in which it will perform consistently.

As with any system, this one is not hard and fast. It is simply a rough indicator, as many factors other than

temperature also play an important part where hardiness is concerned. These factors include altitude, wind exposure, proximity to water, soil type, the presence of snow or existence of shade, night temperature, and the amount of water received by a plant. Factors such as these can easily alter a plant's hardiness by as much as two zones.

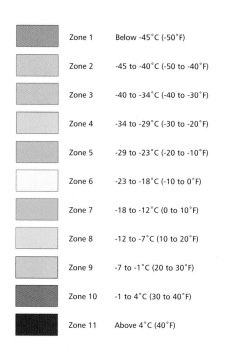

	Zone 1	Below -45°C (-50°F)
	Zone 2	-45 to -40°C (-50 to -40°F)
	Zone 3	-40 to -34°C (-40 to -30°F)
	Zone 4	-34 to -29°C (-30 to -20°F)
	Zone 5	-29 to -23°C (-20 to -10°F)
	Zone 6	-23 to -18°C (-10 to 0°F)
	Zone 7	-18 to -12°C (0 to 10°F)
	Zone 8	-12 to -7°C (10 to 20°F)
	Zone 9	-7 to -1°C (20 to 30°F)
	Zone 10	-1 to 4°C (30 to 40°F)
	Zone 11	Above 4°C (40°F)

Acknowledgements

Unless listed below, photographs are © Anness Publishing Ltd t=top; b=bottom; c=centre; r=right; l=left
RICHARD BIRD PLANT PICTURES: 21br; 23tr; 24tc; 25tl; 25tr; 26br; 30tl; 40br; 41b; 52tl; 52tc; 52bl; 52bc; 56bl; 57tc; 57bl; 61bl; 61br; 66tr; 67b; 69t; 70tr; 76tr; 81bl; 85cb; 88tr; 91bc.   **GARDEN PICTURE LIBRARY:** All pictures Garden Picture Library/photographer: 20tl /Eric Crichton; 22bl /David Cavagnaro; 24tl /John Glover; 24tr /JS Sira; 24bl /Chris Burrows; 32tl /Eric Crichton; 32bl /Bjorn Forsberg; 32tr /Brian Carter; 32br /David Askham; 37tr /Mel Watson; 39bl /Kim Blaxland; 43tl /Howard Rice; 43tr /David Cavagnaro; 44br /Howard Rice; 45tl /Philippe Bonduel; 45tr /Chris Burrows; 45br /Chris Burrows; 46br /Chris Burrows; 51tr /Chris Burrows; 53t /Sunniva Harte; 55t /Howard Rice; 56tc /Eric Crichton; 57tr /Howard Rice; 58b /John Glover; 60tl /Howard Rice; 60bl /David Cavagnaro; 63tr /Jerry Pavia; 68b /Brian Carter; 71br /Howard Rice; 74tl /JS Sira; 75b /Marijke Heuff; 79tl /Sunniva Harte; 82tr /Jerry Pavia; 82bl /Chris Burrows; 84tr /John Glover; 84br /Brian Carter; 85tr /John Glover; 85bl /Mark Bolton; 85br /Juliette Wade; 86tr /Howard Rice; 86b /Friedrich Strauss; 87t /Marie O'Hara; 87b /Didier Willery; 89br /Howard Rice; 92br.

The publishers would also like to thank:
Peter Anderson and Ray Cox for their work on the photography and Unwins for giving access to their grounds for photography.